Identity and Play in Interactive Digital Media

Recent shifts in new literacy studies have expanded definitions of text, reading/viewing, and literacy itself. The inclusion of non-traditional media forms is essential, as texts beyond written words, images, or movement across a screen become ever more prominent in media studies. Included in such non-print texts are interactive media forms like computer or video games that can be understood in similar, though distinct, terms as texts that are read by their users. This book examines how people are socially, culturally, and personally changing as a result of their reading of, or interaction with, these texts. This work explores the concept of ergodic ontogeny: the mental development resulting from interactive digital media play experiences causing change in personal identity.

Sara M. Cole is a filmmaker and independent scholar. She teaches media and culture courses and makes low-budget movies in Baltimore, Maryland. Her newest class, The Language of Politics, will be offered through Osher at Johns Hopkins University in Spring 2017. Dr. Cole's past publications address concepts of gender representation and connections between work and play.

Routledge Advances in Game Studies

Identity and Play in Interactive Digital Media

Ergodic Ontogeny

Sara M. Cole

Routledge
Taylor & Francis Group

LONDON AND NEW YORK

First published 2017 by Routledge

2 Park Square, Milton Park, Abingdon, Oxfordshire OX14 4RN
52 Vanderbilt Avenue, New York, NY 10017

Routledge is an imprint of the Taylor & Francis Group, an informa business

First issued in paperback 2019

Library of Congress Cataloging-in-Publication Data
CIP data has been applied for.

ISBN: 978-1-138-22900-6 (hbk)
ISBN: 978-0-367-88536-6 (pbk)

Typeset in Sabon
by codeMantra

This book is dedicated to my siblings, Anna and John, who let me wake them up early on weekends to try to beat *Zelda* all in one go.

Contents

List of Figures and Illustrations

Preface

The ideas presented in the following chapters are the culmination of an investigation that began in 2010; they follow my research through the development of a new term that more fully encompasses the complexity of new media influences on identity. The literature included are those that informed my conceptions of interactivity, immersion, player agency, and ergodics during these years as I explored the varied disciplines that contribute to the field of video game studies and considered future directions of inquiry. The progression of my thoughts on these topics, my findings after conducting interviews with players, and reflexive critique of the research process are shared to suggest a view of interactive media theory that is informed by multiple analytical perspectives and values results on the individual level.

My first experiences of video game play occurred at other people's homes on the Nintendo Entertainment System and Atari. Interactive digital play via these apparatuses was in mixed-gendered groups with content that challenged my previous (non-video game) play habits. Later games, such as *Duck Hunt* (1984) or *Mortal Kombat* (1992), engaged competitive thematic content that was absent from most of my other playtime. Early discourses of digital play, regarding the potential to try on new characters and identities, were part of the allure. This may have inspired an early curiosity for how this particular type of entertainment or creative practice provides social space for play by both male and female gamers. Yet, the dominant incentive for play was the desire to compete on an equal level with other players regardless of game content and narrative themes.

My first home video game experience was the computer game *The Oregon Trail* (1971), educational to an extent as the player's motivation is to complete a journey west during the settling of the frontier, a simplified retelling/re-enactment of this time in American history. The predominantly text-based game requires decision-making regarding food, animal care, repairs to the wagon, and disease. Upon receiving a Super Nintendo, video games' allure shifted from agentive choice (I did not appreciate games like *Myst* (1993) at the time of their release, for instance) to an almost obsessive desire for mastery and completion of levels of action with overarching story elements, but clear and attainable short-term goals. Games like *Super Mario World* (1990) and *The Legend of Zelda: A Link to the Past* (1991) met these desires for immediate reinforcement with longer-range narrative elements that correlated well with my other play habits, which relied heavily on storytelling and narrative imagination.

Though players may be unaware of the event of *reading* an interactive digital text, like a video game, in the same way they would consider the act of reading a book, magazine, or text-based information from the Internet on a computer screen, reading is still very much taking place. This is a specific kind of literacy that is even more deeply involved with identity and ideology construction due to immersion in the game world and a sense of personal agency during play. Video games represent the future of storytelling, changing the impact of cultural narratives in important ways through a process of learning and internalization of game content that alters players' perceptions of self and reality.

Continued rigorous research of interactive media is necessary because of the speed at which technology changes its capabilities and the dominant nature of its format. It is how many people will tell, hear, and experience stories, culture, and values. I establish a theoretical and methodological approach that defines elements of what it means to play in this interactive digital format and study the influence of game-play on thought and behavior for an initial sample of interview participants. This book is intended for readers who work in the video game industry, media analysts looking for a more sophisticated appreciation of video games beyond mainstream celebrations and rejections, scholars looking for evidence of a more complex explanation of interactive digital play, mass media organizations searching for a means of concisely expressing the nuanced realities of the ways video games change individuals, and video game players, like me, who feel under- or misrepresented by one-sided analyses. Background information from past theorists and concrete examples are included for readers less familiar with the research topic to create an accessible text with a broader audience in mind.

The writings of theorists in ludology, ergodics, and interactive media narrative studies that led to the present text are included in each chapter to allow the reader to follow my logic as I argue for a combination of research approaches and more clearly defined terminology. The blending of this traditional book format with a comprehensive level of detail for non-experts and linked video examples (via URL and QR Code within this text) is an essential reflection of my thesis. A single approach is not enough to fully, accurately, and authentically address any question or research problem, and discursive disciplines must be used together in new media studies. Only through an acknowledgment of the merits (and limitations) of both popular and academic notions of video games can we truly begin to discuss the complex meaning of individual identity and ideology construction as a response to interactive digital play—that is, *ergodic ontogeny.*

Recent shifts in new literacy studies expand definitions of text, reading/viewing, and literacy itself. The inclusion of non-traditional media forms is essential. Texts beyond written words, images, or movement across a screen are ever more prominent in media studies. Included in such non-print texts are interactive media forms like computer or video games that can be understood in similar, though distinct, terms as *texts* that are *read* by their users. This is not an arbitrary metaphor. Media forms communicate in very intentional and specific ways that are understood according to reader/player/user's understanding of this communicative act. The concept of ergodic ontogeny explores the influence of these shifts on identity construction. How are people socially, culturally, and personally changing as a result of these experiences?

This text aligns theoretically with the works of James Paul Gee in his use of language to explore inclusive definitions of texts and media influence as well as Ian Bogost's work on critical video game studies. A somewhat comparable edited volume is *The Video Game Debate: Unravelling the Physical, Social, and Psychological Effects of Digital Games* (Kowert & Quandt, 2015). However, ergodic ontogeny approaches the interdisciplinary call to define the effects of interactive media from a more theoretical and directed approach. This book explains past perspectives on interactive media literacy and suggests which concepts we ultimately need to combine to reach a more comprehensive understanding of individual developmental processes, and therefore sociocultural shifts, that are a direct result of the ways in which players experience interactive narratives.

My previous publications serve as grounded theory forming the theoretical foundation of ergodic ontogeny (Cole 2013, 2014). The interview content presented here is drawn from these works, which focused on linguistic data about the internalization of interactive media narratives. I use *identity* to denote the sense of self resulting from new knowledge/experiences, and investigate the influence of game play in an immersive, agentive, virtual environment as influenced by ludic play theory, character/avatar identification, narrative, and computer/game programming. The acceptability of interactive entertainment media as qualified for rigorous academic study has improved in recent years, though a stigma still exists to a certain extent, and authors often relegate games to a sub-category of new media digitization. However, new literacy studies as developed by Gee (2002), Kress (2008) and others, support the idea that the plethora of immediate and unavoidable experiences of popular culture plays a role in personal development. The influence of these literacies unavoidably extends to identity construction, which again is informed by digital literacy. How do people know and understand the semiotic cues around them?

I began with in-depth interviews of a purposive snowball sample of young adult men who grew up playing video games, beginning with the Atari or Nintendo Entertainment System (NES), and who self-identified as continuing gamers into adulthood. This is the first generation of people in the United States to grow up with video game technology available for home use and who are familiar with each iteration of video game console as graphical interfaces, haptic feedback, and narrative detail improved. Primary themes emerged from these interview data, the details of which are broken down through pragmatic analysis in later chapters. These themes include gender identity and normative discourses of masculinity, experiences of immersion in digital interactive play, the importance of narrative (story, dialogue, and plot progression), and the critical differentiation between experiences of the real and the virtual. Based on these specific themes, I situate my argument for ergodic ontogeny within the broader scope of new media studies. I argue for a necessarily interdisciplinary methodological approach to understanding interactive digital media, and a more cohesive analysis of video game influence that incorporates and balances multiple views according to play theory, ludology, narratology, and ergodic theories.

The pragmatic analysis of specific language-use included in this book is merely a single lens through which interactive media influence individuals' perceptions of themselves and others. Discourse analysis provides a foundation for themes of ergodic ontogeny that will be further established through future research. Individual aspects of this project could easily be studies of their own. This could take the form of analyzing a specific population in terms of age, gender, culture, socio-economic status, or any other criteria that might provide an acute analytical lens. Similarly, the content of the interviews could be explored in terms of personal response to any one aspect of interactive digital game play: the narrative of specific games, senses of player agency, connectedness to avatars and playable/non-playable characters, online interactions, expressions of self within interactive play in terms of gender or other descriptors, and so on. Textual analyses of games themselves provide insight into possible social influences, cultural expressions and representations, potential associations with violence, or any other number of criteria. However, rather than writing a book that only used sociolinguistics, or focused only on visual literacy, game mechanics, the influence of cultural trends, or a content analysis of U.S. media coverage of interactive entertainment media or other topics, this book argues for a combination of approaches. Before we can attempt an explanation of interactive media influence on individuals through such pursuits, it is essential to establish the overall elements of analysis and then ask specific questions of each part of the whole.

The first chapter begins by establishing the need for rigorous study of interactive digital gaming, provides specific examples for readers who

may be less familiar with the strides in related fields over the last decades, and addresses news media coverage of this rapidly advancing and
extremely popular medium. News coverage often focuses on potentially
destructive psychological influences of gaming, but there are some exceptions. For example, *Minecraft* (2011) is considered educational, and
used in some schools to help students become more focused, organized,
and future-thinking. The content of *Minecraft*, however, is different
from most bestselling video games that often rely on adult-oriented imagery and content. Such discrepancies beg the question: is the process
of playing video games beneficial in teaching people to think? Is the
content of games problematic? Is the predominance of single-player and
online game play a concern for future socialization? It is easy to see why
people are both concerned and encouraged by the potential influence of
this medium. Conceptions of play, agency, and interactivity support an
interdisciplinary approach to thinking about new forms of digital literacy, shifts in conceptions of the human versus computer, and the ways
we understand the differences between the virtual and real world. The
first chapter concludes with a description of the process by which the
new term *ergodic ontogeny* was derived and what it is meant to imply.

   To fully understand the methods inherent in researching the ergodic
ontogenetic process, Chapter 2 provides a foundation for play theory.
Play theory provides varied and contentious definitions of *play* that support specific delineations between work and play and between experiences of the real and virtual. Based on these discursive accounts of
play, a more refined definition of new media and interactive play through
digital technology leads to a discussion of interactivity and definitions
of the *player*.

   Player or user (of interactive media) is a complex term. It could imply one
who is taken along for the ride by the intentions of the programmer, or on
the other hand, one who discovers and even creates ergodic experience as
play happens. An introduction to immersion and realism in games leads to
a more detailed discussion of uses of the term *interactivity* that draws on
Espen Aarseth's explanation of cybertexts. Aarseth's term, *ergodic* literature, denotes the non-trivial effort required to traverse a computer/video
game as text. Ergodic theory provides the final component to interactivity
by describing how a player moves through a coded computer program, as
opposed to reading a book or watching a film: the specific experience of
human interaction with computer-generated game systems.

   The second chapter concludes with an analysis of theories of
human-computer interaction, delving deeper into the connection between player and game continued in Chapter 3 in a discussion of
computer-mediated communication (CMC) and discourse (CMD). My
review of new media and digital literacy includes a self-aware critique
of the ways in which academics discuss new media. Discussions of simulation, representation, and ergodic literature establish video games as

a unique media experience in which representations of cultural symbols and personal identity markers are mediated through the computer or television screen. Simulated expression influences the effects of multi-modal and computer-mediated communication on players.

Emergent themes of distancing and denial in masculine discourses of games are evidenced in the interview data provided in Chapter 3. Descriptions of interview data and the interview process itself inform a discussion of highly personalized conceptions of play, especially in terms of a computer/digitally mediated narrative, expressed by participants as a distancing of video game play experience from reality. The way players relate to game experiences leads to a discussion of computer-mediation of narrative elements. Narratology supports the importance of story to our cultural myths and the sharing of social mores. In games, narratology explores text-based story elements, dialogue, and plot (programmed and coded progression of game play) in relation to a game's overall content, social themes, cultural expressions, character development and association with the player, and potential for immersive experiential play through a predetermined storyline.

The relationship between narrative and play is described in detail in the fourth chapter. Video games are a form of cultural narrative: an expression of narrative imagination or taking the perspective of others. Chapter 4 includes a critique of the use of literary and film terms as foundational terminology for video game studies. Key distinctions between video game narrative and other forms result from non-linear storytelling and the cultural influences of gaming, ludology, and interactivity. The interview data in Chapter 4 is coded and analyzed according to pragmatics. The discourse demonstrates themes of heroic protective discourse that situate games as an outlet for aggression and competition as well as a means of finding catharsis in the mundane aspects of real and/or virtual experiences. Players report acting out social needs or desires in virtual realms.

Interview analysis suggests an internalization and personalization of ideologies expressed through console games. Games with narratives that specifically include overt moral decision-making are investigated in terms of narrative game play and programming. Narrative/plot, incentive processes, dialogue trees, and character creation are addressed. Players experience, rather than observe, the narrative in video games, a crucial distinction between this and other media forms. Chapter 4 concludes with a description of video games as experiential narrative (in support of the conclusions drawn from interview analyses) due to active engagement of the player through feelings of agency in games.

The internalization process resulting from interactive media experiences is the essence of ergodic ontogeny. Chapter 5 confirms the importance of player experience through sociolinguistic analyses of discourse reflecting specific identity and ideology markers. Interview examples in this chapter support complex constructs of gender self-identification in terms of male hegemonic structures in Western culture and related social expectations to meet those stereotypes in play, work, and other parts of life. This data suggests that identity and ideology construction rely on players' connections with characters, levels of immersion in digital/ virtual environments (though this does not necessarily imply realism), actions, narratives, and the associations expressed between virtual and real world authenticity.

Players internalize interactive digital play experiences in ways that are informed by their knowledge of the relationship between games and reality. New media technologies change our sense of self (both real and virtual), our conception of what it means to be human, and what interactions with in-game characters and environments mean in terms of real world consequences (if anything). Concepts of the post-human and the nature of digital environments help to illustrate how these factors influence the efficacy of ideologies embedded in and shared through games. Chapter 5 ultimately returns to a discussion of the importance of the player in light of these additional considerations.

The final chapter continues the discussion of the value of player experience as elucidated through qualitative interdisciplinary research and provides detailed insight into the methodological decisions made in the previous chapters. I critique the interview process, choice of participants, and method of analysis and discuss the importance of self-reported data, pragmatic analysis of discourse, and critical concern for the reasons behind decisions that informed my analyses. Finally, a self-reflexive critique of the writing process is presented. Feminist research methods and considerations of hierarchies of power through the research process bolster reliability and validity and explain the rationale supporting modifications to traditional research formats for readers expecting a project that conforms more directly to their disciplinary understandings of the term. I mention my personal perspectives on data analysis, inclusion of past literature, and the writing process itself throughout the book, but this section of Chapter 6 addresses the process more directly and in additional detail. This need for reflexivity in fieldwork, data collection, analysis, and writing and the inclusion of participants (including yourself as a reader) as equal constructors of knowledge is paramount in the content as well as the form of this work.

For example, additional data will be collected from those who read this book or happen upon some of its content online and choose to comment. Many of the links and QR Codes in this book lead to video examples that contain citation information for the games or images presented and (just below that information) a question about the subject of the video. These questions invite comment from anyone who views them. Responses are collected for future analysis. Though many aspects of this book follow traditional formatting requirements, there are some requisite directions for use. Readers of the print version of this text may access links with a QR Code similar to the image in Figure 0.1.

Figure 0.1 QR Code Example. https://vimeo.com/ergodicontogeny.

To access QR Codes while reading this document, a smart phone or other mobile device is needed. Scanning the image with a QR scanner application will connect the referenced website. In this example, scanning the QR Code links to the main page for the Ergodic Ontogeny video site.

Emergent themes of identity and ideology are established through examples from a case study on masculine discourse. These themes are explored in connection with past theoretical work in play, narrative, and ergodic literature. This book provides a basis for continued research and thought. It is intended as a foundation for future discussion. Cultures share meaning through narratives. I suggest that as our social narratives become interactive, digital, and self-selected, individuals' ontogenetic development (a term borrowed from psychology) will be inherently altered due to ergodic experiences (ergodics used in an expanded and inclusive form compared to that of Aarseth's original work regarding non-trivial effort).

A deeper understanding of what play experiences mean must rely on interdisciplinary lenses of analysis that value player reports, programming choices, immersive experiences, technology advances, and cultural narratives equally. I hope that the field will continue to expand and embrace alternate explorations of interactive media affect. The European Research Council grant to Espen Aarseth at IT University of Copenhagen (2016) will allow, it is hoped, for continued, rigorous work in this area. The value of this line of inquiry is only beginning to be recognized in academia and research centers around the world. Clear terminology and broad appreciation for the complexity of analysis necessary for such endeavors are essential components to progressing our understanding of interactive media influence.

Acknowledgments

This research benefited greatly from discussions at numerous conferences and is indebted to the University of Maryland system for grants for funding travel that provided opportunities for me to meet new international communities of artists, programmers, and academics who expanded my conceptions of new media theory. I would like to thank Melissa Hilbish at Johns Hopkins University for supporting my early investigations of unexpected media reception and influence and Beverly Bickel and Craig Saper at UMBC for their guidance as my work transitioned to interactivity, simulation, and play. Stuart Moulthrop at the University of Wisconsin-Milwaukee has been a great resource and inspiration during my research and writing processes, as well.

I am grateful for the thoughtful insights of interview participants from all past projects, without whom I wouldn't know where to start. Early versions of analyses and interview data were published in *Special Issue: New Works on Electronic Literature and Cyberculture* (2014) and *Interculturalism, Meaning, and Identity* (2013). I thank the editors for permission to draw from these articles. Thanks also to Gerhard Boomgaarden, Felisa Salvago-Keyes, and Christina Kowalski at Routledge for their help navigating the publication process.

This project advanced thanks to conversations with numerous colleagues and mentors and most of all thanks to my dad for long phone calls about the best way to get at ideas of identity development from within and outside individuals (ontogeny). I also thank Dan Pittore for years of moral support and technical expertise. This research is ongoing, and I cannot adequately express how much I appreciate the patience, love, and encouragement of my mom, dad, and the rest of my family and friends as I continue to pursue new ways to understand who we are (or think we are) and what makes us that way.

1 Ergodics and Ludology

There is no limit to what you can do, where you can go...you can really escape into the game... You know, I am a Marine Corps veteran. Having been to Iraq and experienced real battle...when I was playing that video game, I mean, I actually dreamt about my service during that time, you know. And (laughs), I'll tell you what, I haven't had a vivid dream like that since right before, since right when I came home.

—Levi

What are the limits of virtual experience? Do they exist in the minds of players? Do they bleed into everyday life beyond the subconscious level, beyond our dreams? How do moments lived through game narratives or ludic elements of play physically enacted via a hand-held controller relate to identification and psychological development beyond the game world? The complex relationship between the *virtual* and the *real* is experienced through narrative, play, and interactivity by players who report contested expressions of self, cultural stereotypes, and reasons for and results of playing video games.

Video games and other forms of interactive entertainment change storytelling, which changes the influence of cultural narratives. Representations of video games and players run the gamut from the acne-ridden obesity of *South Park* characters locking themselves in basements playing *World of Warcraft* (2004) to cartoonish claims regarding game content on national news programs[1] and *Pokemon Go* (2016) players walking themselves off cliffs or into traffic. Few critics embrace a nuanced approach to understanding video game influence. The complexity of this still relatively new medium must not rely on ill-informed, opinion-based exaggerations. A deeper understanding of how people play video games and what these play experiences mean must be addressed through interdisciplinary lenses of analysis that value player reports, programming choices, and cultural narratives equally.

The current text provides background information for readers unfamiliar with the various subjects included. This level of detail is still relevant for advanced students as interactive media study is a relatively new field being pushed in many complex, interdisciplinary directions. This book explains past perspectives on interactive/digital literacy and suggests which concepts should be combined or rejected in order to reach a more comprehensive understanding of the individual developmental processes, and therefore sociocultural shifts, that are derived from the ways we experience interactive narratives. Reorienting the field of interactive media studies to be more subject-driven is crucial. Expanding and reworking definitions of *literacy* and *text* are also essential goals.

Players are often categorized as strictly interested in rapidly incentivized violent actions or quickly processing visual and aural cues to solve puzzles and navigate virtual environments. Players themselves report that, although interest in such elements is often present, they use games to keep in touch with friends, work through emotions that are difficult to express publicly, and enact varied social or psychological roles. Video games influence individuals through an internalization of game content that alters players' perceptions of self and reality. The findings presented here do *not* support a connection between this internalization and social concerns such as increased violence or de-socialization. Players recognize the allure of supposedly *negative* elements of video game play[2] but ultimately express a decided disconnect between the real world and virtual experiences of play.

Video games, like other popular media in the past, come under regular criticism by news organizations, media critics, and politicians. Many analyses focus on the potential for game play to increase aggression, violence, and shortened attention spans[3] and blame video games for negative outcomes in society.[4] The following chapters present a theoretical approach that defines elements of what it means to play video games and evaluates current analytical tools for studying the qualitative influence of game-play on thought and behavior. This book synthesizes diverse conceptions[5] of interactive digital media in pursuit of common themes reflective of video games' influences on personal identity and ideology.

The content of this book catches the reader up on theories from previous decades, exploring video game influence through discussions of play theory, narratology, game programming, and interaction with video game hardware. The following chapters incorporate essential theoretical aspects of new media in cultural terms and draw on emergent themes based on sociolinguistic analyses of interview data. The term *ergodic ontogeny* is introduced, which incorporates disparate theories floating in various disciplines, and begins to concretize critical components that contribute to identification through video game play. Ergodic identification is the sense of self resulting from this developmental process.

Future academic endeavors must incorporate multiple analytic approaches into the study of interactive digital media.[6] The present text identifies basic themes of interactive media influence based on interview data, locating the emergent themes from participants in past theories of interactivity and play. The construction of identity through ergodic ontogeny relies on players' connections with in-game characters, levels of immersion in digital/virtual environments, feelings of player agency through actions and narrative, and the crucial differences between experiences of the virtual and of the real. Though some video games may look or feel very real,[7] the ideological and identity construction that takes place is distinct from real-world experience in important ways that allow for the internalization of new personal and cultural knowledge as shared through the veil of virtual experience, as opposed to real, and an understanding of the differences between the two. This inherent and necessary complexity inspired the need for a new comprehensive term for the developmental process associated with interactive digital play—ergodic ontogeny.

1.1 Ergodics and Ludology

Cultural and personal identity formation and ideological construction are inherently tied to (new and old) media consumption. In the last 30 years, a new entertainment form excelled in terms of sales and scope—video games.[8] Forms of interactive entertainment media are available for free on smart phones, are playable online in public spaces,[9] and make up a dominating industry with billions of dollars in profit each year in the United States alone.[10] If entertainment media silently, or at least covertly through the guise of simple pleasure if not outright propaganda,[11] influence the ways in which we understand who we are and how we relate to the world around us, it is of utmost importance to find clear and detailed ways of analyzing this new interactive medium as player agency (the feeling of control over a character or other elements of the play environment) leads to increased internalization of cultural data.

Aside from individuals[12] who attack video game play for personal or political gain, interactive entertainment media products are often relegated to the realm of being *just games*. This oversimplification results in overreactions by uninformed consumers when the effects of the medium are called into question. Despite efforts by the Entertainment Software Review Board[13] (ESRB) to implement a self-scaled ratings system, similar to the ratings for films, many parents ignore warnings and purchase video games for children regardless of adult content, likely because the word *game* is in the product description.

The multiple uses of words like *game* and *play* are detailed in the discussion of play in the next chapter. Ignorance of these terms leads to a demeaning of the medium, primarily due to its association with and widespread adoption by youth in modern society. Like print, film, comic books, and television before them, video games are often overlooked until there is a problem that might be linked to their consumption.[14] Instances of violence in children, for example, may seem high, but causes are certainly multi-determinable.[15] With adoption by the United States military[16] and other institutions, it is increasingly indisputable that the interactive element of video game play leads to a form of training of the player. Training has long been associated with simulations, but as computer graphics improved and merged with entertainment, the line between *playing* and *learning* blurred.

As a game is played, the level of difficulty increases to accommodate increased skill by repeat players. This trend emerged during the arcade years of video game play but is a common element to any competitive activity. Could this train the player to need ever-increasing stimuli? Interactive entertainment media are repeatedly singled-out as possible causes for increased aggression or violent tendencies, and sources like newspapers and websites often flood the market with sound bites from academics condemning them. The critics who are most video game friendly admit the limitations in methodology and data, which often reflect the goals of the researcher rather than the realities of the player or of video game studies.

Is content alone to blame for players who take violent behavior in a game-world into a real-world setting? Does the playing of a game matter or will watching someone play that same game content have a similar effect? How do variables like age, culture, and gender[17] influence the results? These questions cannot be answered quickly or easily and are difficult to squeeze into a succinct sound bite in response to a tragic event for which video games might be blamed.

Another side of interactive media research involves pedagogical applications of new media technology and our ability to exploit the shift to computer-mediated learning. The difference between traditional teaching methods (lecture/note-taking) and interactive experiences (either with digital components or without, such as playing with other children) is a rapidly growing field of research. Informed by theories of critical pedagogy, educational approaches that position students as active participants in the learning process are often effective.[18] Digital technology provides a variety of learning methods that involve the transfer of information as a means of sharing "knowledge as a process of inquiry" (Freire, 1970, p. 58). Creative digital processes allow students and teachers to learn about a subject together, forming a learning environment in which they communicate more effectively and co-construct knowledge to create change. Education that allows for sharing of personal experience, expression of the individual, and the ways in which students relate to, are influenced by, and create society as they see it in their daily lives, facilitates an approach to learning that values the voice of teachers and learners equally (Gee, 2007; Giroux, 2003). In a virtual learning environment, students may even take the lead and surpass traditional authority figures while taking ownership of their own academic curiosity.

Most people in the United States interact with digital technology numerous times each day, the necessity of which is becoming more and more prevalent. Educators want to foster the use of technology for critical thinking and collaboration as well as for creativity and play (Czarnecki, 2009). Students with exposure to digital technology[19] at an early age, especially those who have the opportunity to continually engage in digital learning processes, will be more prepared to negotiate a highly digitized environment. Drotner (2008) argued that the social divides of digital competency at a young age strongly influence future social stratification; technical knowledge may well be the key to future competence in a "globally digitized society" (p. 68).

The educational aspect of interactive entertainment media is often categorized as something other than a video game. The term *video game* most commonly implies an interactive form of digital entertainment, either downloaded or available on a disc, played with a joystick or controller on a computer or television screen with little or no redeeming educational value, a stigma that still plagues research in this field as assumptions are quickly made regarding studies about a topic as trivialized and divisive as video games.[20] There is a clear contradiction in the popular use of the term *video game*. It seems relevant to ask how the same artifact/text that is blamed for *teaching* aggression or *training* killers has limited educational value. Is it simply the plot of a game that determines whether it is detrimental to its player or a welcome asset? Are educational games necessarily void of competition or increased stimulation of their players' senses? Why do people in the United States and other countries around the world continue to consider games with violent content most enjoyable, based on sales and ratings? How do we value research on these subjects? How might all of these factors be understood in conjunction? These questions are beyond the scope of any individual project, and my interest is not to prove or deny links between video games, learning, and conceptions of violence, but to expand our means of discussing such topics through qualitative research and theoretical exploration. By clarifying certain elements of the process of interactive media influence, members of all disciplines will be better able to work together to fully analyze these complexities.

The *texts* analyzed in this book are video games. They are also described as interactive digital media products or *interactive media*, a term that sets them apart from other new and traditional media forms without including the words *video*, which is inaccurate, or *game*, which is often misunderstood and devalued. Interactive entertainment media is not limited to computer or console games, especially considering the widespread use of hand-held gaming apparatuses and cell phone games. It encompasses any medium that allows for player/reader/subject interactivity. Alternate reality games, virtual simulations (whether they conform to a game system or rule-based and goal-oriented framework or not), and other forms of digital virtual reality fall into this category as well. The present thematic analysis is limited to one type of interactive digital media (single-player console games), but the terminology regarding media effects is applicable to all forms that have an ergodic component of player agency.

The goal of academic explorations of video games should be one of demystification.[21] A video game is not a board game, book, film, or computer program (in the strictest sense). Though technology is an integral component of interactive digital entertainment, there are many non-technical elements that are equally crucial to the play experience, such as aesthetic and aural cues, plot, character, and player.[22] Of course, these aspects are created by and shared with the player via the physical, technological apparatus of a computer or game console, so the physical nature of the hardware cannot be ignored. The player must make decisions to advance the story, and this sets video games apart. Importantly, decisions are informed by a combination of visual, aural, digital/technical, and tactile (in the form of rumble pack controllers and more recently motion sensors on consoles) cues built into the programming of a game.

Analyses of specific game experiences in cultural terms are often based in either ludology, narratology, or ergodic theory. Ludology (derived from Latin *ludere*, meaning to play) is the study of games and gaming. Ludology focuses on the specific elements of games themselves and their processes such as rules, actions, expectations, and interpersonal interactions. It is not limited to video games or particularly concerned with topics such as interactivity with computer systems or immersion in digital virtual environments, though recently the field has come to encompass these traits as well. Specific elements addressed by ludology, such as rules that govern game play or how players engage certain game strategies, fail to fully explain the personal and social influence of play experiences that take place via current interactive entertainment media such as console or computer games.

The process of ergodic ontogeny bridges the gap between ludology and narratology, valuing both simultaneously as equally relevant to our understanding of digital interactive play experiences. Narratology focuses on the plot of the story that the player is told, discovers, or co-creates. Narratology is often applied to interactive and new media studies, especially story-driven video games. Narrative is a crucial component in many video games. The inclusion of improved graphics often yields increased cinematic qualities of cut-scenes and game play, as well as higher expectations from players for an enthralling story to accompany these visuals. Narrative elements and ludic outcomes are necessary, but not sufficient, for an exploration of video games. A third essential theoretical component, *ergodics*, is required. This word is perhaps less easily deduced by readers unfamiliar with human/computer interaction theories.

Derived from Greek *ergon* (work) and *hodos* (path), Espen Aarseth borrowed the term ergodics from the fields of math and physics and introduced it in relation to computer games in *Cybertext: Perspectives on Ergodic Literature* (1997). Aarseth used *ergodic* to refer to the effort required to complete a computer game's story and (or via) its rule-based systems and goals. This encompasses both narrative and ludic elements of play.

Interactive digital media force players to perform with a certain amount of effort, something different from mere *attention* on the part of the player. The player must make choices, solve puzzles, or react within a dictated interval of time to an in-game/on-screen stimulus. This effort advances the game and, at the same time, draws attention to the choices that a player chose *not* to make: puzzles that were avoided or reactions that were a second too late. Interactive digital gaming is a unique medium in that its narrative structure requires non-trivial effort to traverse a *text*. The artifact is a game, and the player/user/(w)reader[23] is aware of the path not taken. Players must act. This added component of intention and feeling of agency sets ergodic texts apart and increases their levels of influence on participants.

Emergent themes in interview data provide the foundation for a discussion of moments of player agency with moral/ideological development opportunities. Players reported that video games serve as outlets for aggression, competition, relaxation, and friendship. The data reflect an internalization of game narrative by players due to the increased level of involvement necessary to experience this medium. Player agency is evoked in these lived-through virtual experiences. Modern digital game play, narrative, and programming/coding require new definitions of play and specific terms through which to analyze moments of influence (Moulthrop, 2005).

Are games art?[24] Can we simply borrow the methods and terms of literary criticism or film studies and apply them to interactive digital entertainment forms? Modern video games are more than text on a page or television screen; agency draws players into an immersive play environment. They are also something other, arguably more than and different from film. Cinema studies value narrative, sound, and aesthetics, and are therefore a useful starting point for some game theorists. However, when watching a film, the viewer is told a story and watches it unfold through the moving images on the screen. There is, with very rare exception in the early days of DVD or perhaps recent experimental interactive art installations,[25] an opportunity to personally interact with the film as the viewer. We do not determine what happens in the next scene or which characters, paths (both narrative and literal), or opportunities are pursued while others are ignored. In an interactive digital video/computer game, however, players have this agency and ability to alter their course, at least within the limits of the game's programming.

Video games fall, for most people, comfortably into the realm of *distraction* as dubbed by the Frankfurt School (Horkheimer & Adorno, 2002). They are influential forms of meaning-making that exploit the evocative potential of immersive digital media and change depending on the person experiencing/enacting/performing them. This requires a new set of terms (ergodics being a primary example) developed in recent decades and also a new combination of methodologies that encompass the layered simultaneous participatory events that take place in any moment of modern video game play. These layers of experience are present within single-player gaming, often referred to as *story mode*. Experiences of play expand and change through online or multi-player gaming. The case study data presented in this book concerns single-player console gaming and supports a theoretical discussion of the influence of digital interactive play on players. The analysis begins with emergent themes from interview responses of individuals who grew up playing video games and who often deny any recognition of direct influence of interactive media on their cognitive and emotional development.

Concepts of morality, gender self-identification,[26] aggression, competition, and cognitive stimulation through video games may influence players' conceptions of *right* and *wrong*. Yet, play certainly includes a sense of the unreal, *playing at something* rather than doing it in seriousness. If so, how do players value ideologies that are knowingly developed through play? Morality and ethics are highly localized, determined by the cultural and social mores and values of one's community, family, and country. Does the understanding of what is moral, ethical, or just seep beyond the virtual experience of playing an interactive game into decisions made in reality (non-virtual environments) with real people?

Aggression as the product of entertainment such as viewing a film, reading a comic book, experiencing a video game or card game, or playing sports is heavily debated. Do video game players react with more aggression after play? Is this a result of narrative content with moral over-/undertones? Is it due to the competitive nature of games that almost always have a goal system in which players must succeed as opposed to fail, progress rather than remain still? Is aggression increased in other aspects of life after video game play or does the play experience at times serve as an outlet for feelings and physical or cognitive needs? Do feelings, ideas, and personal identification experiences during interactive digital play remain after the game experience ends?[27]

The analysis of people's talk about game-play experiences included in this book supports the complexity of causes for personal identification and ideology construction through interactive entertainment. Many video game narratives rely on traditional heroic story arcs, acting as rifacimentos of morality plays or fables for the modern era. Through interactive digital media, player agency provides moral/ideological identity development as well as an outlet for aggression/competition (Cole, 2013, 2014).

Mass-marketed, as well as underground/open-source, gaming is an art form that must be explored rigorously by academics of all disciplines and consistently updated as new technologies emerge. It is essential that we problematize the often-binary arguments of game studies (ludology vs. narratology, for example, or mentally stimulating vs. mentally erosive). The nuanced influences of digital experiences and the new ways of knowing that are developed through interaction with such media require multi-lensed analyses pulling from various disciplines in order to form the most robust conclusions.

Current academic and professional discourses regarding interactive entertainment such as computer or console gaming are varied and unresolved.[28] Whether ludic programs have narratives, or are simply feedback loops of data systems in computer hardware and human brains, depends on an author's or theorist's personal stance on what aspect of digital game play qualifies as the object of study. Ways of gauging the influence of interactive digital play are equally varied, as evidenced in studies over the last decades that often lack compelling results in any particular direction (Anderson et al., 2010).

What seems clear is that as interactive media become more and more prolific, people will acclimate to their specific modes of communication and reflexively acquire new vernacular and understandings of visual and other cues. This is what Ulmer (2002) referred to as electracy—the navigation of new media through digital literacy. How does this new literacy change personal conceptions and ideologies? Does the medium matter in terms of entertainment outcomes and influences on individuals' understandings of themselves and the ways in which they choose to interact with others? "Literacy researchers have shown that readers do read popular culture texts as forms of mass culture, using the text as a kind of manual for constructing identity" (Hagood, 2008, p. 534). Players take broader meaning and applications from information that is shared with them through video games, whether they notice when it happens or not.[29] Cultural artifacts are read and interpreted depending on the social climate, challenging certain assumptions and redeeming others, as well as players' correspondent identity markers.

Conceptions of ergodic literature and games as popular cultural *texts* rely on analyses of design principles, programming, and the fostering of player agency. Play theory explores how this new form of literature/literacy relates to traditional conceptions of play in society. As game programming becomes increasingly complex, elaborate webs of narrative potential require a means of talking about digital interactive play as more than ludology (games and rules). New media literacy incorporates predefined disciplinary concepts, but lacks cohesive and comprehensive terms for talking about some aspects unique to interactive digital play.

A broader conception of play is necessitated by the proliferation of sandbox games[30] that provide nearly endless possibilities for individual experiences and interactivity as well as nuanced moral narratives through aspects of play that do not meet traditional definitions of gaming (gamification[31] of real life or mundane activities is an example of this). The ways in which these shifts in play experiences and interaction with digital technology alter perceptions of self, culture, and knowledge/learning require examination. Such an examination must rely on current conceptions of humanity in relation to automata/robotics and computerization of lived experience as virtual reality and full-body physical engagement in games becomes more common.[32] This examination must also focus on personalized responses to play as they manifest in self-identification and ideological development of individuals interacting with others in virtual and non-virtual spaces.

This book repeatedly alludes to three key aspects of video game research: ideas of play, agency, and digital interactivity. Video game play "engenders modes of interaction and attachment between player, system and game world that differ from detached, vicarious viewing... the player is locked into the circuit-loop of the system and views their on-screen representation not as an independent entity...but rather as a set of potentials, available techniques, opportunities and capabilities which can be embodied" (Newman, 2002, p. 418). We play video games, rather than watch them as one does a film. We must follow rules, operate within the potential of the programming available, solve puzzles, or accomplish tasks within these parameters, and have a goal beyond the narrative (if there is one) either to accomplish completion of the game or to sate our own curiosity through exploration of the game world. Most games are played to win, whether this means completing the available narrative, exploring an environment in its entirety, reaching a high score, or mashing the correct combination of buttons until all enemies are defeated. Regardless, due to the connection to the actions of onscreen representations, players are invested in this media form on a more personally involved level.

The ways in which this embodied potentiality is shared via the artifact of the game itself shape the player on a personal level. Using "Hine's (2000) notion of cyberspace as both culture and cultural artifact," Thomas (2008) explained that "understanding cyberspace involves understanding culture—that is, the politics and meanings (Bakhtin, 1981) inherent in cybercommunities, and the subject positioning of the members within them" and "it [also] involves understanding cultural artifacts...that shape the communities" that use them (p. 671). Cyberfeminist studies, such as Haraway (2003) and Braidotti (2003), used discourse analysis, media, and cultural studies to discuss the many facets of cyberspace and culture. Similarly, this book draws on themes established through discourse analysis of segments of interview data to explore the cultural, social, and personal facets of interactive media play experiences.

Identity is a complex concept in games, in the real world, and in between. Though a player may choose to take on the physical appearance of a character in a video game that is nothing like the person playing, the decisions made and ideologies followed while playing still reflect some elements of that individual and his or her personal ways of knowing (Gee, 2007). The influence of technology on individuals is established in games through feelings of player agency. The game interface is a "continuous interactive feedback loop, where the player must be seen as both implied and implicated in the construction and composition of the experience" (Newman, 2002, p. 410). Self-consciousness is also a crucial component. "According to the simple flow of energies into and out of the registered interface, there is no 'feel,' yet players demonstrate and report corporeal experience. Classical HCI [human-computer interaction] studies...cannot accommodate such non-registered inputs/responses" (Newman, 2002, p. 415). This means that players may not notice when they respond physically to virtual sensations, but they do. Human-computer interactions that are not in the form of interactive digital entertainment or agentive play do not elicit the same user reports. Interestingly, a common side effect of being told about such non-registered responses is that players attempt to inhibit such movements/reactions, adding yet another layer of complexity to self-reported data (Newman, 2002). Immersion in a play experience may not result in increased authenticity in feedback from players.

Interactive digital media are increasingly narrative-driven, incorporating characters with whom players are meant to identify, though certainly some games are "regimens more than experiences. Tools more than art. Drills more than challenges" (Bogost, 2011, p. 141). The differences and similarities between those types of game experiences and ones that are more narratively focused must be explored in terms of plot structure as well as player agency in relation to identification and ideological expression. Bogost (2011) argued that rather than continuing to attempt to grasp at overarching theories of game analysis, "we need more media entomologists and media archaeologists...to find and explain the tiny treasures that would otherwise go unseen" (p. 148). This is very true and informs the plans for additional future research expressed in the final chapter of this text—finding the details to complete the whole. Video games do not exist solely as unique experiences. There are certainly trends and overarching concepts that may be applied to many interactive experiences within a given genre. These themes inform and direct detailed research to come.

1.2 Making a Case for Interdisciplinarity

Situating the exploration of interactive digital play across disciplines and methodologies provides an opportunity to collaboratively create a deeper, more complete understanding of how such media operate in societies, in this case the United States, and supports an approach to scholarship that functions in connection with other researchers and epistemologies in order to pursue the most timely and thorough analysis possible. Media scholars often reference concepts of digital literacy and electracy[33] but often lack consistent definitions across disciplines and individuals. It is necessary to elucidate shared meanings within analyses of interactive digital texts, discourses of players/users' experiences of these media, and the networked programming/software that forms the games themselves.

This book builds from the findings of a qualitative case study using cultural studies, ludology, narratology, sociolinguistics (pragmatics and discourse analysis), and gender theory (hierarchies of masculinities, gendered popular cultural expectations) to provide an interdisciplinary context for a humanities-based analysis of the influence of digital interactive play on personal and cultural understandings. Though other research[34] includes biomedical data from video game players, hypotheses here will draw directly on emergent themes established through discourse analysis.

Narrative influences the construction of personal identity and ideology via interactive digital media. Narratives operate in unique ways in this medium. At issue is the complex nature of narrative itself and its effect on the reader/player/user of a text.[35] Interview data provides context for experiences of narrative through virtual interactive play. Gender self-identification, moral ideologies, sociocultural understandings, emotional and psychological development, and hierarchies of masculinity/ femininity are all components of this process. New media literacy informs players' abilities to foster close relationships with characters in game worlds. These play experiences engage feelings of player agency that, in turn, inform individuals' moral and ideological development. The ways in which players, whether referred to as actors, performers, agents, or even writers, understand these experiences provide meaningful insight into how they identify with the characters they manipulate in digital environments and the kinds of connections they make between reality and the virtual world.

Player discourse provides the initial analytical lens for identity and overt moral decision-making in interactive play that informs a deeper understanding of player identification and development of player agency. Morality is especially subjective and culturally localized. Participants' personal definitions of moral decision-making, identification, and experiences of reality are expressed in their interview responses. Additionally, various video games are discussed as the most common or traditional approaches to game narrative and programming or as helpful counter-examples.

1.3 Discourse Analysis

New media theory provides a framework to explore the ways in which culture, socialization, and access to power change as digital media advances. Technology is influenced by and influences the relationship between entertainment media and personal identity construction. Methods of cultural analysis must value personal involvement in cultural creation at individual levels. Interactive digital games require player input, making the player an integral part of video games' very existence. The ways in which players express experiences during and after gameplay help elucidate the influence of this process. My analysis of ergodic ontogeny begins with player discourse analyzed according to pragmatic discourse analysis. This discourse also provides feedback regarding the narrative structures and themes of certain games.

The case study that serves as the thematic foundation for this work provides linguistic analyses of shared thoughts on digital interactive video game play (Cole, 2013, 2014). Participants of similar age and professional background completed in-depth interviews that lasted between one and three hours. Discourse analysis explores the ways language expresses conceptions of identity and understandings of cultural influences on lifestyle, self-identification, and speech.[36] All names included in this book are pseudonyms chosen by the participants themselves. The anonymity of interviewees helps to support an interview environment in which research participants feel comfortable sharing details of their personal lives that sometimes support and are sometimes at odds with traditional or popular values in United States culture.[37]

The questions addressed in the interviews explored the ways in which exposure to a variety of interactive digital entertainment, at a young age and continuing to adulthood, influences personal conceptions of right and wrong, gender identity, and cultural understandings. Participants discussed the types of games they played and still play, how they felt about those experiences as children and adults, why they felt compelled to enter the career field they did, how they believe the two might or might not be related, and their perception of influences on everyday values and identification that might result from interactive media play. The structure of the interviews began ambiguously in order to avoid leading participants toward any preconceived hypotheses. Toward the end of the interview session, questions were more pointed regarding connections between earlier topics, asking participants to relate ideas that they might initially dismiss having any connection.

Participants were informed that all identifiable information about them will be confidential at all times. The inclusion of questions specifically about their personal feelings and beliefs required that this point of confidentiality be made clear.[38] Participants contributed their own thoughts in response to questions, at times prompting a tangential exploration of experiences not outlined in the original interview. This freedom of expression is ideal for a linguistic analysis of discourse because it allows participants to speak more naturally. Participants that are directly quoted in this book provided discourse that was representative of the group as a whole, and was the clearest example of trends noticed in the interview responses overall. Interview transcripts were coded thematically, and these themes informed the approach to analysis of ergodic ontogeny through concepts of ergodic, ludic, and narrative theory.

Interactive entertainment media require active involvement of players that leads to individual experiences of play. Increases in availability of technology afford players the opportunity not only to play games that they purchase from large companies, but also to support smaller independent ventures or even create their own digital games. This shift results in individuals having a higher level of influence on the culture industry in terms of accountability, trends, and potential for social action than ever before. Public response to interactive media reflects social trends. Media industries, however, still dominate the market and shape cultural identities and ideological predispositions through the products they create. The reciprocal nature of the relationship between the *media industry* and the *individual* requires an analytical approach that considers both texts (games) themselves and the experiences of those who play them.

Layered iterations of texts in experiences of interactive gaming are not bound by literary convention. Networks of narrative potential lead to more complex evocative influences as well as greater variation in audience response. As Clifford and Marcus (1986) suggested, media forms evoke rather than represent ideas and signify a depth of experience at any given moment. New media complexity adds *player agency* to this already inherently personal process, which informs personal identity development and cultural awareness. Introspection is essential for exploration of not only cultural productions but the concepts behind these seemingly innate structures.[39] Culture must be explored from within.

Through the interdisciplinary approach provided here, analyses of texts and discourses form a more complete understanding of interactive media influence on how we form and share personal identity and cultural beliefs. *Electracy* is shifting modes of communication and expanding academic analysis into invention and creation (Ulmer, 2002). Player experiences, and their *talk* about these experiences, inform the ways in which shifts in communication influence individual's understandings of their own identity construction and the influence of virtual reality and play on real life.

Using a pragmatic discourse analysis method (Cameron, 2001; Cutting, 2002), sections of interview transcripts are broken down in terms of word choice and sentence structure. Any pauses or laughter, deep breaths, code switching, or other linguistic devices are considered in terms of probable meaning and potential relation to individual identity and ideological discourse attributes of the participant (Scheuer, 2003; Van Dijk, 2006). In the excerpts from transcription, the following visual indicators are used: the letter I references the Interviewer, (#) during discourse indicates the seconds of pause between speech acts, 1. 2. 3. on the left indicates line of discourse for analytical reference in the next paragraph, // indicates any overlap or interruption, <u>underlined</u> text indicates emphasis on certain syllables or words, ?s indicate uptake, :: indicates drawn-out speech, and (.) indicates a clear pause.

The following is an excerpt from one interview that includes the relevant coding and analysis. Copper described his experience playing *Double Dragon 2* (1989) as a child. Copper (C) described the game in terms of its narrative content.

Copper's response:

1. C: Uh (.) Billy's girlfriend in Double Dragon 2 gets kidnapped (.)
2. C: or murdered (.) I forget which (1)
3. C: because I think she comes back at the end in a really ridiculous cinematic.
4. C: And then he enlists the aid of his brother (.)
5. C: cuz you know, that's what you do.
6. C: My girlfriend's dead, you want to go beat the hell out of every thug in the city?
7. C: I mean, su::re?
8. C: Why n::ot (.) What are friends for?

The plot and game play of *Double Dragon 2* is provided in abbreviated form in this video (scan QR Code in Figure 1.1 for video from archive.org) with the girlfriend character clearly positioned as an object of desire (note her clothing) and the incentive for action (through her inaction and death).

The sarcasm noted due to the speaker's stress of words like "that's" (line 5) and "sure" (line 7) at the end of the statement implies that he is using hyperbole in his reference to beating up every single criminal in the entire city and that this expectation of machismo is either outdated or overrated. This act of distancing takes on a personal tone of

Figure 1.1 Screenshot of *Double Dragon 2*. Double Dragon 2: The Revenge [Video game]. (1988). Tokyo, Japan: Technōs. https://vimeo.com/185106348.

Figure 1.2 Screenshot of *Double Dragon 2* game play. Double Dragon 2: The Revenge [Video game]. (1988). Tokyo, Japan: Technōs.

disapproval that masculine ideologies extend beyond the fantasy setting of the game to real-life expectations. Copper cannot recall whether the girlfriend lives or dies; she is inconsequential to the process of game play, only returning in a "ridiculous" (line 3) graphic at the end. The defeat of enemies is paramount in this play experience.

Researchers must include the player in a theory-based cultural analysis of interactive media forms to attain a more complete picture of the influence of digital gaming. Ong (2002) argued that digital literacy avoids personalization of information, which implies the distancing that a screen and game controller might create between narrative and player. Another distancing aspect of this form of interactivity involves shifts in human consciousness that rely perhaps too heavily on visual and narrative cues. New media moves knowledge into the realm of the visual, interactive, and immediate. Technology changes quickly. Researchers must update and re-evaluate analytical tools and the texts to which they are applied. Through an analysis of past approaches to game studies and discourse analysis of players' talk, a deeper understanding of current trends may be realized.

1.4 Problems with Definitions

The term *ergodic identification* is used by Carr (2006) to differentiate identification with characters in video games from identification that takes place with characters in a film. She builds on Aarseth's use of ergodics to mean the need for *nontrivial effort* to traverse or read a text/game/virtual experience. This connection to the character on the screen is an important element of identification with virtual experiences; however, the agentive quality of interactivity overall is a form of identification as well. All ergodic elements influence the player in fundamental and unavoidable ways. When grappling with terminology for this elusive, yet obvious, process, I began with a concept of *ergodic identity* rather than *identification*—something I mean in a different way from Carr's usage. Building on the notion of ludic identity, established by de Mul (2005), which explored the cultural and personal influence on identity resulting from ludic experience (playing games), I defined ergodic identity as the identity that a person establishes after a transformative experience of digital virtual play.

My use of ergodic identity (rather than identification) is not the way in which the person/player identifies with the avatar on the screen during game play, though that is certainly relevant. What I mean to imply is the change that occurs within the player during and even more after video game-play experiences. It is the change in worldview or shift in ideology that might occur due to a *lived* experience that would not be possible in the *real* world. Identification is a necessary, yet insufficient, prerequisite to the evolution of identity. de Mul's ludic identities encompassed parts of this shift in ideology in terms of the rule-based, incentivized processes of game play that exist outside of game worlds (gamification). However, shifts in personal identity and ideology, ways of understanding oneself and others, and the relationship between oneself and the world are part of a more personalized process.

Should this be described as a post-ludic ideology shift? Ludology's focus on the action/event aspects of game-play neglects the importance of narrative and other thematic elements. A more open term is needed. Ergodics, in my opinion, allows space within its own definition for play theory, ludology, narratology, and game mechanics. The non-trivial effort Aarseth described was initially applied to the requirements imposed on players through computer programming. Because of this, it points to the game itself and all that comes with it in modern new media, digital, narrative-based play experiences. Game programming is all of these things combined, creating an immersive moment for players to identify with the characters on the screen or the first-person view of the play experience through which they are navigating (Carr's ergodic identification).[40]

This sense of realism and agency alters personal identity and ideology beyond the play experience. My definition is less concerned with the broad cultural implications that gaming may have on individuals—ludic identity—such as playful identities or expectations of gamification in other aspects of society. I am interested in personal, unnoticed, or perhaps quite obvious at times changes in meaning-making as a result of video game play. This involves shifts in epistemology, consciousness of the *real* versus *virtual*, the ways we view the world around us, our ideas of morality, and how we interact with one another.

This is not to imply that playing a game necessarily changes who we are. But it is to say that it can and may. This is well established in media studies—viewers identify with a character and therefore gain new perspectives on their own lives and ideas about the world. It is crucial to our valuing of this media, especially as it has become the most profitable and prolific in U.S. culture, to look at how ideology may or may not be influenced by such experiences and how even violent,[41] frightening, and troubling play may lead to more complete knowledge of players' own thoughts and feelings with relatively mundane, and at times cathartic, outcomes for players.[42]

The term *ontogeny* is borrowed in the field of psychology from biology to denote "the ways in which the organism relates its inborn needs to environmental demands" (Campbell, 2009, p. 693).[43] The idea of personal mental and emotional development as *influenced by* and *influencing* its environment sets this concept apart, and is therefore useful in distinguishing the post-play identification I am describing from traditional cultural/social constructs of terms like *ludic identity*. The term ontogeny, personal mental development as a result of one's environment *and* one's role in that environment, can be re-appropriated to imply the changes in mindset or understanding that occur during game-play, navigating and reacting to and with the virtual environment. Ludic ontogenesis, therefore, would involve the changes in mindset/understanding resulting from game-play as one navigates a virtual program or rule-based environment, but it does not imply ontogenetic development applied to the world outside of that particular game experience. Ludic ontogenesis culminates in de Mul's ludic identity and is ultimately a precursor to that concept. Combining the concept of ergodics with this individualized developmental process provides a single point of departure to discuss the personal mental shift resulting from the complex experience of video game play.

The combination of terms most adequate for my work here is *ergodic ontogeny*. Ergodic ontogeny, in my definition, is the personal mental development resulting from interactive digital media play experience. This results in ergodic identity, defined as the sense of self (moral, ideological, epistemological) that results from new knowledge/experiences through game play in an immersive, agentive, virtual environment that includes the influences of ludic play theory, character/avatar identification, narrative, and computer/game programming. Carr's ergodic identification is a part of this process when players identify with the characters they control on the screen. Expanding Aarseth's term to encompass the multiple elements of digital interactive play provides a comprehensive descriptor for the developmental process explored in this book: ergodic ontogeny. The following chapters will address how play theory informs our understanding of agentive and emergent play experiences in interactive digital entertainment, how interactive entertainment/distraction is valued as a form of meaning-making, how these conceptions must be updated to reflect a more nuanced sense of video games' influence, and how players exploit the evocative potential of immersive technical media through layered iterations of texts. In other words, how do players *use* games and how does this influences the effects of their play experience?

Notes

1 See http://youtu.be/PKzF173GqTU for a clip from Fox News in 2008 regarding the game *Mass Effect* that evokes themes of gender discrimination and social discomfort with sexuality in U.S. culture and harkens back to arguments reminiscent of the Hollywood Production Code that limited media content through direct censorship.
2 See this ad for *Dead Space* that promotes a generational divide to a very likely young male audience (http://youtu.be/nKkPFDEiC6Q).
3 Most media coverage toggles between ill-informed condemnation of games for causing violent tendencies or scandalizing children's morality (for instance, the criticism of the *Grand Theft Auto* series, games not intended for underage audiences), lauding gaming as therapeutic or pedagogically superior to traditional methods (see *Operation Supply Drop* http:// operationsupplydrop.org/ regarding games to treat PTSD during wartime), or the idea that non-violent games having any actual entertainment value is newsworthy (see *Mother Jones* article http://www.motherjones.com/ media/2013/09/12-totally-kick-ass-violence-free-video-games).
4 Video games operate within a social context that is positioned in terms of dominant narratives that exist and are propagated through media, inter-personal communication, and cultural knowledge. Media, especially video games most recently, are cited as cause for anti-social behaviors or achievement failures. However, the social fabric of our cultural narratives influences all creative possibilities, as well as the technology through which these possibilities are expressed, and our interactions with each other that are mediated by them. The discussion of video game influence cannot ignore the sociocultural realities within which media exist and must recognize that many of the broader issues at the core of social concerns (such as violence, education, morality) are more complex and are at times ignored in favor of a specifically identifiable artifact (a video game) with thematic content that references, but does not necessarily cause, the larger concern. Additionally, one of the most common topics of criticism involves video game contents' influence on children, an audience for which many games are not intended.
5 This includes mainstream media, play theory, narrative analysis, ludology, human-computer interaction/discourse, ergodics, and discourses of play, gender, and ideology as expressed through in-depth interviews.
6 As required by ergodic ontogeny, a single angle of analysis is insufficient.
7 Even if not, they may have very real messages that influence their players/ audiences.
8 Speaking in 2011, Jane McGonigal is quoted, "Currently there are more than half a billion people worldwide playing computer and video games at

least an hour a day and 183 million in the U.S. alone. The younger you are, the more likely you are to be a gamer; 99% of boys under 18 and 94% of girls under 18 report playing video games regularly. The average young person racks up 10,000 hours of gaming by the age of 21 or 24 hours less than they spend in a classroom for all of middle and high school if they have perfect attendance" (very high numbers though the term *regularly* is arguably disputable) (http://www.ted.com/conversations/44/we_spend_3_billion_hours_a_wee.html). Recent shifts include digital gaming increases via mobile game platforms. The National Purchase Diary (NPD Group) noted a decrease in gamers overall in 2012 (https://www.npd.com/wps/portal/npd/us/news/press-releases/pr_120905/) and an increase in online gaming (https://www.npd.com/wps/portal/npd/us/news/press-releases/the-npd-group-report-shows-increased-number-of-online-gamers-and-hours-spent-gaming/) in 2013.

9 Free Internet (usually wireless) connectivity is available in most cities in the United States in hotels, fast food restaurants, coffee shops, and libraries.

10 Video game revenues for 2015 were roughly $23.5 billion (see http://www.theesa.com/article/u-s-video-game-industry-generates-23-5-billion-in-revenue-for-2015/).

11 Such as commercials, political messages, etc.

12 A prominent example from 2007 is Jack Thompson, a high profile video game opponent. For more information, see http://www.jackthompson.org/.

13 See www.esrb.org for more details and the most recent ratings of new game releases.

14 The shooting at the U.S. Navy Yard in Washington D.C. on September 17, 2013, for instance, mentioned in most initial coverage (within the first 24 hours) that the shooter played violent video games; other media habits were not mentioned. Al Jazeera reported he was *obsessed* with violent games (this link to the original report has since been removed http://america.aljazeera.com/watch/shows/live-news/2013/9/alleged-navy-yardshooterob sessedwithviolentvideogamessaysfriend.html), CNN reported on his play of shooting video games (http://www.cnn.com/2013/09/16/us/dc-navy-yard-gunshots/), ABC noted military style video games (http://abcnews.go.com/US/navy-yard-shooter-aaron-alexis-angry-frustrated-vengeful/story?id=20276128), and a Fox News host stated that there should be a registry to track video game purchases and play times due to their risk factors (during *Fox & Friends* morning show on September 17, 2013).

15 See Robertson, McAnally, & Hancox (2013) and Wilson (2008).

16 Video game play is used for training but also recruitment purposes. See http://www.goarmy.com/downloads/games.html.

17 We must view these concepts, especially those most contested (gender) as analytical categories, not just identities, in "an attempt to find new avenues into the dense and complicated problem of explaining the extraordinary persistence through history and across societies of the subordination of women" (Acker, 1990, p. 145), the potential devaluing of experience of the very young or very old, and the relegating of male emotions to limited cultural stereotypes.

18 Social movements often suggest that "not merely play and games but life itself is supposed to be fun" (MacCannell, 1976, p. 35). Is there necessarily a distinction? If attention and idea formation are traditionally thought of in ways that are no longer relevant to the modes in which modern society accesses and shares information, then it is necessary not only to investigate media and the specific content of particular data, but also the self-reported

influences of this media on the individual. Are people truly distracted or can this be a more effective means of meaning-making? Is play dominating work or is leisure time being overcome by new types of work that go unnoticed or are misunderstood?

19 These might include cell phones, tablets, or personal computers with constant Internet access and the ability to text or video message others; touch screens in place of other forms of interactions at banks, stores, or restaurants; and robotic assistance. This is an issue of communicative competence in an increasingly digital, technology-reliant world, a question of digital literacy.

20 A vocal counter-example is Jane McGonigal, who suggests that "games can boost our resilience, help us experience post-traumatic growth, and even give us 10 extra years of life" (see http://janemcgonigal.com/ for details of her research.).

21 Clifford and Marcus, in *Writing Culture* (1986), argued that there is no objective culture to be found and analyzed. Culture, especially with the advent of new media convergence, has more and more sides—a puzzle that becomes all the more complex as interconnected systems have increasing access to one another through technology. We must let go of the notion of a single author, as the contributors to *New Media/New Methods* (2008) asserted, and move toward an exponentially layered discussion that is not bound by literary tropes but analyzes culture while creating new iterations of that very thing. As Clifford and Marcus (1986) explained, it is the "whole point of evoking rather than representing" that frees ethnographers from restricted modes of analysis (p. 130). The difficulty is finding representational models that signify the depth of experience in any given moment. New media, with its immediacy and levels of complexity especially in online spaces, is perhaps our best option.

22 Interviews with video game writers, such as Tom Bissell (*Gears of War*), provide interesting insight into this process from the perspective of game creators (Bustillos, 2013). See http://www.newyorker.com/online/blogs/books/2013/03/gears-of-war-writer-tom-bissell-on-video-games-and-storytelling.html.

23 The hypertextual combination of writing and reading that implies input from the user of a text in its understanding, and therefore creation, built on Ulmer's (2002) work on *electracy*.

24 Walter Benjamin's work, for example, makes a clear distinction between distraction and concentration in terms of media consumption and illuminates the ways in which technical media merge the two (Benjamin & Arendt, 1986). Through constant overlapping of associations, spectators are both distracted and forced to concentrate at the same time during the viewing of a film, for instance. New technologies continue to exploit this evocative potential of immersive technical media, relying on audiences being removed from the *art object* itself in its original incarnation. We now experience reproductions/replays of the art, allowing viewers to be constantly reminded and aware of the medium itself. Benjamin argued that this awareness translates beyond entertainment into knowledge and social awareness. Semiotics and aesthetic codes are difficult to define, culturally contextual, and subjective, but are of critical importance because this form of social interaction and communication "constitutes the individual as a member of a particular culture or society" (Fiske, 2010, p. 2).

25 Machinima, the combination of machine and cinema, is a counter-example that "refers to the process of creating real-time animation by manipulating a

video game's engine and assets… [that] allows users to explore, create, and connect with their favorite games in new ways" (http://www.machinima.com/overview).

26 My interest in gender self-identification is not strictly in terms of femininity or masculinity, but in the relationship between the two. This perspective moves beyond the fight against biological determinism and looks at "the physical itself as a social construct" as a "social category of analysis" (Fonow & Cook, 1991, p. 216).

27 Interactive digital entertainment is both a product and a cause of new ways of thinking, reading, and speaking. New neural networking processes may demonstrate this shift on a physical level, as will be posited in an outline for future research in Chapter 6.

28 For example, a *New York Times* article cited meta-analyses that support the correlation between media violence and violent actions, but pointed out that despite these factors there is no clear causation or lack thereof, and that many important questions remain unanswered (Kambam, Pozios, & Bender, 2013).

29 As Hagood (2008) stated, "the shift to more inclusive and expanded definitions of texts (Flood & Lapp 1995), of reading (Gee, 2007; Kress, 2003), and of literacy (Heath, 1991; Lonsdale & McCurry, 2004) that incorporate visual and communicative aspects into traditionally print-focused views has opened up space for the study of non-print" (p. 531). In exploring the meaning behind our production via a given medium, we may better understand the structures and models under which we operate at all times. The "acknowledgement that literacy develops not only by cognitive but also by social and cultural factors has provided opportunities to study how literacy is socially situated, culturally constructed, and dependent upon uses of texts within communities" (Hagood, 2008, p. 532). Gaming communities have strong in/out group affiliations and operate within a complex social context of media literacy, teetering between being valued as the newest frontier of communicative forms and the stereotyping of play as mere frivolity. Situated understandings of new media literacy illustrate how games relate to social and learned behaviors. Entertainment media is as relevant as other sociocultural processes, but must be valued accordingly as only one element of influence on an individual's development within their own cultural space.

30 This term refers to video games with large open areas that players may explore with great levels of freedom. Examples of sandbox games can be found at this comprehensive blog: http://www.sandbox-games.net/.

31 Gamification refers to the process of applying ludic elements to everyday activities, such as a points system for brushing teeth or eating the suggested servings of daily vegetables. A TED talk discussion of this concept can be found here: http://www.ted.com/talks/jesse_schell_when_games_invade_real_life.html.

32 Minsoo Kang's *Sublime Dreams of Living Machines* (2011) explored the concept of humans in terms of mechanical creations in the form of automata intended to mimic the human form. Similarly, Hayles' (1999) analysis of the posthuman relationship between human thought and computerization is telling of the possibilities that new media and technologies afford and also of the assumptions we bring based perhaps on historically situated logocentrism that has permeated our thoughts over thousands of years of writing culture.

33 See Ulmer (2002), *New Media/New Methods: The Academic Turn from Literacy to Electracy* (Rice & O'Gorman, 2008) and *Inter/vention: Free Play in the Age of Electracy* (Holmevik, 2012) for additional considerations of this concept and its applications to modern notions of literacy and culture.

34 A number of interesting projects explore virtual reality's influence on perception through medical, scientific means. For example, Jane Aspell's recent work links visual representations of heartbeat to self-perception and out-of-body experience (see http://www.psychologicalscience.org/index.php/news/releases/visualized-heartbeat-can-trigger-out-of-body-experience.html).

35 See Barthes (1977), Bruner (2002), and Hazel (2008).

36 The ways in which play activities of male children with violent, traditionally masculine, themes influence adult interpretations of tolerance to real violence, aggression, and personal identification was explored in my previous work (Cole, 2013).

37 The analyses in the following chapters draw on interview data from male participants who grew up in the 1980s and early 1990s on the east coast of the United States, and are now between the ages of 25 and 35 years. This limits generalizability, but allows for a more focused comparison of participants' responses. The small snowball sample provides data to identify overarching themes within players' discourse. Participants were all active in a career in law enforcement, the military, or a related field in which a certain level of exposure to violence of different kinds is expected, within the last decade. This initial purposive sample was chosen to exemplify men with daily experiences in *reality* that might mirror those found in violent video game play, one of the most widely stereotyped aspects of masculine discourse and most widely criticized aspects of interactive digital gaming (Cole, 2013, 2014).

38 Participants were permitted to decline answering any questions they did not feel comfortable with during the interview process.

39 See Ong (2002) and Rice & O'Gorman (2008).

40 See also Carr's (2006) conception of the avatar as Freudian double.

41 A relationship between the game world and real world is the foundation for popular media and academic arguments correlating video game violence and acts of real-life violence perpetrated by people whose lives certainly involved more than simply playing games before they acted.

42 Gee (2007) described the learning that takes place through video game play in terms of critical pedagogy for deep learning. He described three types of identity: virtual (the character in the game that one embodies in the virtual realm), real-world (the player), and projective (projecting values onto the character and the character as a project). The value of these identities outside the game experience functions by taking on new identities and learning to question identity, seeing oneself in new lights, and trying on new roles. Ergodic ontogeny addresses the development of real-world (the player in the world outside the game) identity and how it is altered through all of the identity processes that Gee described.

43 The borrowing of the term *ontogeny* in psychiatry includes developmental stages of object relationships as well as ego development (Campbell, 2009, p. 693–694). The psychological aspect of ontogeny is useful in a discussion of ergodics. My assertion is that a developmental process of identification and understanding occurs through individuals' experiences of ergodic texts, an experience that must be analyzed according to multi/interdisciplinary perspectives.

References

Aarseth, E. J. (1997). *Cybertext: Perspectives on ergodic literature.* Baltimore, MD: Johns Hopkins University Press.

Acker, J. (1990). Hierarchies, jobs, bodies. *Gender & Society, 4*(2), 139–158.

Anderson, C. A., Shibuya, A., Ihori, N., Swing, E. L., Bushman, B. J., Sakamoto, A., ... Saleem, M. (2010). Violent video game effects on aggression, empathy, and prosocial behavior in Eastern and Western countries: A meta-analytic review. *Psychological Bulletin, 136*(2), 151–173. doi:10.1037/a0018251.

Barthes, R. (1977). Image, music, text. In S. Heath (Ed.), The photographic message (p. 15–31). New York, NY: Hill.

Benjamin, W., & Arendt, H. (1986). *Illuminations.* New York, NY: Schocken Books.

Bogost, I. (2011). *How to do things with video games.* Minneapolis, MN: University of Minnesota Press.

Braidotti, R. (2003). Becoming woman: Or sexual difference revisited. *Theory, Culture & Society, 20*(3), 43–64. doi:10.1177/02632764030203004.

Bustillos, M. (2013 March). On video games and storytelling: An interview with Tom Bissell. *The New Yorker Blogs.* Retrieved from http://www.newyorker.com/online/blogs/books/2013/03/gears-of-war-writer-tom-bissell-on-video-games-and-storytelling.html.

Cameron, D. (2001). *Working with spoken discourse.* London, UK: Sage Publications.

Campbell, R. J. (2009). *Campbell's psychiatric dictionary.* Oxford, UK: Oxford University Press.

Carr, D. (2006). *Computer games: Text, narrative and play.* Cambridge, UK: Polity.

Clifford, J., & Marcus, G. E. (1986). *Writing culture: The poetics and politics of ethnography.* Berkeley, CA: University of California Press.

Cole, S. (2013). Discourses of masculinity: Culture, identity and violence. In D. Boswell, R. O'Shea and E. Tzadik (Eds.), *Interculturalism, meaning and identity* (p. 153–164). Oxford, UK: Inter-Disciplinary Press.

Cole, S. (2014). Gender identity construction through talk about video games. Special issue:New works on electronic literature and cyberculture. *CLC Web: Comparative Literature and Culture, 15*(16.5). Retrieved from http://dx.doi.org/10.7771/1481-4374.2487.

Cutting, J. (2002). *Pragmatics and discourse: A resource book for students.* New York, NY: Routledge.

Czarnecki, K. (2009). Chapter 3: How digital storytelling builds 21st century skills. *Library Technology Reports, 45*(7), 15–19.

De Mul, J. (2005). *The game of life: Narrative and ludic identity formation in computer games.* Retrieved from http://www.digra.org/dl/.

Drotner, K. (2008). Boundaries and bridges: Digital storytelling in education studies and media studies. In Lundby, K. (Ed.), *Digital storytelling: Mediatized stories* (p. 61–81). New York, NY: Peter Lang.

Fiske, J. (2010). *Introduction to communication studies.* Philadelphia, PA: Taylor & Francis.

Fonow, M. M., & Cook, J. A. (Eds.). (1991). *Beyond methodology: Feminist scholarship as lived research.* Bloomington, IN: Indiana University Press.

Freire, P. (1970). *Pedagogy of the oppressed* (trans. Myra Bergman Ramos). New York, NY: Continuum.

Gee, J. P. (2007). *What video games have to teach us about learning and literacy* (2nd ed.). London, UK: Macmillan.

Giroux, H. A. (2003). Public pedagogy and the politics of resistance: Notes on a critical theory of educational struggle. *Educational Philosophy and Theory,* 35(1), 5–16. doi:10.1111/1469-5812.00002.

Hagood, M. C. (2008). Intersections of popular culture, identities, and new literacies research. In J. Coiro, M. Knobel, C. Lankshear, & D. Leu (Eds.), *Handbook of research on new literacies* (p. 531–551). New York, NY: Taylor & Francis.

Haraway, D. (2003). *The companion species manifesto: Dogs, people, and significant otherness.* Chicago, IL: Prickly Paradigm Press.

Hayles, N. K. (1999). *How we became posthuman: Virtual bodies in cybernetics, literature, and informatics.* Chicago, IL: University of Chicago Press.

Hazel, P. (2008). Toward a narrative pedagogy for interactive learning environments. *Interactive Learning Environments,* 16(3), 199–213. doi:10.1080/10494820802113947.

Holmevik, J. R. (2012). *Inter/vention: Free play in the age of electracy.* Cambridge, MA: MIT Press.

Horkheimer, M., & Adorno, T. W. (2002). *Dialectic of enlightenment: Philosophical fragments.* Palo Alto, CA: Stanford University Press.

Kambam, V. K., Pozios, P. R., & Bender, H. E. (2013). Does media violence lead to the real thing? *The New York Times.* Retrieved from http://www.nytimes.com/2013/08/25/opinion/sunday/does-media-violence-lead-to-the-real-thing.html.

Kang, M. (2011). *Sublime dreams of living machines: The automaton in the European imagination.* Cambridge, MA: Harvard University Press.

MacCannell, D. (1976). *The tourist: A new theory of the leisure class.* Berkeley, CA: University of California Press.

Moulthrop, S. (2005). After the last generation: Rethinking scholarship in the days of serious play. In *Proceedings of digital art and culture conference* (p. 208–215). IT-University, Copenhagen. Copenhagen, Denmark.

Newman, J. (2002). In search of the video game player: The lives of Mario. *New Media & Society,* 4(3), 405–422. doi:10.1177/146144402320564419.

Ong, W. J. (2002). *Orality and literacy: The technologizing of the word* (2nd ed.). New York, NY: Routledge.

Raessens, J., & Goldstein, J. (Eds.). (2005). *Handbook of computer game studies.* Cambridge, MA: MIT Press.

Rice, J., & O'Gorman, M. (Eds.). (2008). *New media/new methods: The academic turn from literacy to electracy.* Anderson, SC: Parlor Press.

Robertson, L. A., McAnally, H. M., & Hancox, R. J. (2013). Childhood and adolescent television viewing and antisocial behavior in early adulthood. *Pediatrics,* peds. 2012–1582. doi:10.1542/peds.2012-1582.

Scheuer, J. (2003). Habitus as the principle for social practice: A proposal for critical discourse analysis. *Language in Society,* 32(2), 143–175. doi:10.1017/S0047404503322018.

Thomas, A. (2008). Community, culture and citizenship in cyberspace. In J. Coiro, M. Knobel, C. Lankshear, & D. Leu, *Handbook of research on new literacies* (p. 671–698). New York, NY: Taylor & Francis.

Ulmer, G. L. (2002). *Internet invention: From literacy to electracy*. London, UK: Longman.

you found me. (n.d.). *you found me*. Retrieved from http://janemcgonigal.com/.

Van Dijk, T. (2006). Ideology and discourse analysis. *Journal of Political Ideologies, 11*(2), 115–140. doi:10.1080/13569310600687908.

Wilson, B. (2008). Media and children's aggression, fear and altruism. *Children and Electronic Media, 18*(1), 87–118.

2 Interactive Play

Gee, did you have tea parties, did you play Barbie, Chutes and Ladders, you know, whatever! My Little Pony. None of that stuff, it was mostly guy play. Even when I was playing with my sister it was mostly guy play because it was Star Wars and G. I. Joe.

—George

2.1 Play Theory: A Summary for the Unfamiliar

Children's play constructs worlds that can be deconstructed according to the needs of the player. Adult play may seem inconsistent with more common definitions of play, though it certainly exists despite seeming to "have more to do with waiting than with preparing...with boredom than with rehearsal...with keeping up one's spirits than with depression" (Sutton-Smith, 2001, p. 48). Whatever the impetus, the question remains: are the results of play the same regardless of the characteristics of the person playing? Inevitably, the answer must be no. The personalization of play experiences is precisely the complexity that makes research into the influences of play so difficult to generalize. Children and adults are not so different in the fantasies in which they partake, yet representations of children's play are framed in terms of physical toys, play apparatuses (like jungle gyms), and imaginary play within groups or alone. Modern children's play increasingly relies on the re-mediation of a television, computer, or cell phone screen. The potential for deconstruction by the player is in some ways limited by game programming and technical ability or dependent on socioeconomic or other factors that keep some children from either hardware or Internet access. For large segments of the U.S. population, however, improved technology expands gaming potentials with each new console generation. During play, whether completely within one's imagination or illustrated on a screen, "all players unravel in some way the accepted orthodoxies of the world in which they live, whether those orthodoxies have their source in adult or child peer groups" (Sutton-Smith, 2001, p. 166).

As Sutton-Smith (2001)[1] stated, "our fantasies are the microworlds of inner life that all of us manipulate in our own way to come to terms with feelings, conflicts, realities, and aspirations" (p. 156). As children age, their stories include heroes who master defeat, an extremely common theme in interactive digital gaming that is similar to other risk-taking behaviors that fall into the realm of *play* or *entertainment* for adults. Conceptions of childhood versus adult play are constantly shifting. Adult play increasingly includes interactive entertainment media. The generation that grew up with mass-marketed technology like the Atari and Nintendo Entertainment System maintained involvement on some level with this medium into adulthood. Adult collective play theory often focuses on who is controlling ritual activities of identity creation or discovery. This aspect of play theory is concerned with levels of control and cultural capital: what the person, group, or entity that controls play experiences, traditions, and expectations is getting out of the experience and who is in a position of power as a result. This harkens back to the culture industry, those individuals or organizations with creative control over video game content (plot, visuals, voice-actors) and marketing. Stereotypical expectations of game player demographics dictate many decisions, catering to adolescent males and cultural assumptions about their interests and desires.

Everyone knows what play feels like, but people often find it difficult to describe. Fagen (1981) explained that play is irritating, not in that we cannot understand it, but in that we feel as though we do understand or at least know there is more going on than meets the eye and yet have forgotten or are unsure of how to go about pursuing it (Sutton-Smith, 2001, p. 2). Almost any activity can incorporate aspects of play. The metaphor of play is even more widely borrowed and applied to frivolous or mundane concepts as it is to critical and universal ones. Is play an action or a way of describing certain actions? How do we determine whether or not we are playing? Is there a difference between playing games and playing at other experiences?

Bateson's seminal "Theory of Play and Fantasy" (1955) outlined human verbal communication as denotative, metalinguistic, and metacommunicative. *Meta-communicative signals* (these signals can be trusted, mistrusted, etc.) must be understood to know that we are *playing* at all. This takes on an additional layer of complexity when relating play theory to virtual environments and three-dimensional character models.[2] All involved must agree that play is going on, that what is inside the play frame matters, and that what is outside the play frame does not. If all agree that play happens when interacting within a virtual realm, such as is the case with interactive digital gaming, then we may begin with an expectation of metaphor and influence on the player that will be effectively communicated via this medium.

Play scholarship adds to the overall ambiguity of the term within various disciplines. Some scholars "study the body, some study behavior, some study thinking, some study groups or individuals, some study experience, some study language—and they all use the word play for these quite different things" (Sutton-Smith, 2001, p. 6).[3] Play fighting is often viewed as an extension of power (usually attributed to males), and play as social bonding is often attributed to females. Play is also categorized as a form of *flexibility*, innovation in animals rather than only instinct, which is valued similarly to notions of independence, free-will, and intelligence. Sutton-Smith (2001) argued that "by revealing [the] rhetorical underpinnings of the apparently diverse theoretical approaches to play, there is the possibility of bridging them within some more unifying discourse" (p. 9). Computer/console games engage many of these rhetorics through multimodal interactivity. Rhetorics of play value both intrinsic and extrinsic play functions. This refers to the valuing of the "player's game-related motives for playing" in contrast to the functions that forms of play are "supposed to serve in the larger culture" (Sutton-Smith, 2001, p. 17). This is an important distinction when analyzing the ergodic ontogeny of players as they experience interactive digital play in increasingly realistic and immersive environments with ever-expanding potential for open-world formats. The player is the primary point of analysis in play, not the function of a game, though these two are naturally linked and co-dependent/constructed.

The commonly made connection between play and cognitive development, in terms of practicing and recreating inherited instincts of our ancestors, may be unfounded. After World War II, researchers[4] began experimenting with simulations and player engagement in the classroom as a form of teaching. Play serves functions far beyond rote repetition of instinctual reactions needed for survival. Abilities are not only recalled, but evolve, through play—a process that promotes the sharing of newly developed skills with others. Play rhetorics may not link directly to play activity in every instance, but development still occurs when children are playing, and the complexity of their play increases with age. There is no direct correlation between this development and "social, emotional, and cognitive" age-related development, but "it would be surprising if they did not share and transfer skills back and forth" (Sutton-Smith, 2001, p. 42). Children and adults who are successful in play form lasting friendships, build communities, and extend their social networks as "play successes transfer into their more general social and emotional competencies...successful play experience increases the potential for continued happy playing" (Sutton-Smith, 2001, p. 44).[5]

The choice to accept or deny cultural orthodoxies is innately tied to conceptions of group and personal identity. Play serves a purpose in learning about culture and is also itself a form of ritual while permitting creativity and innovation. Play practices help to establish new identities and form bonds with others that reaffirm representations of self that players find most useful, authentic, or enjoyable. This sounds similar to the experience of identification with an avatar within a game but is meant here to extend beyond that implication. Play experiences allow players to represent themselves, in the in-game moment and more broadly in terms of self-identification grounded in those play experiences, in new ways.

Competition exists in most game scenarios, whether individual or team-based, virtual or real. The element of winning versus losing at a game results in typical, predictable reactions from players.[6] Metaphorically, this operates the same way that is does literally: if an in-group affiliation is overrun by a dominant force, they often take up arms in a traditional fashion and avoid abstraction or unique approaches to competition. Similarly, if a player loses in a video game, contesting occurs by replaying that section of the game until it is beaten/defeated and therefore complete, but one must still operate within the confines and according to the rules of the game.[7]

In computer-mediated play, certain narratives and ideological groupings are bolstered while others remain neglected. The slow progression in recent years toward the presence of counter-narratives in popular games (whether produced as AAA titles or simply widely played indie games) speaks to the undermining of traditional hegemonies, though this is still the exception rather than the norm. *Journey* (2012), *The Path* (2009), *Flower* (2009), and *Thomas Was Alone* (2013) are examples of games with counter-narratives that play with ideas of what it means to be a video game.

Ludology is the study of the act of playing games. The process and purpose of game studies, a disciplinary focus distinct from play theory, is debated "most notably perhaps in terms of ludological versus narratological arguments" (Enevold & Hagstrom, 2009, p. 3). Critiques of

Figure 2.1 Screenshot of *Journey.* Journey [Video game]. (2012). Los Angeles, CA: Thatgamecompany.

narratologists suggest that they carelessly apply concepts from film studies and narratology to the studies of games—a prominent concern of ergodic theorist Espen Aarseth, as well. Ludologists argue that games require specific and unique terms for analysis due to the difference between the elements of game play and other media. Varying definitions for terms like *video game*, *play*, and *interactivity* exist throughout the relevant literature. Newman (2004) collected responses from famous game theorists and laymen alike, which suggested continued confusion in definitions in this field with little resolution. As Aarseth described them, games are "productions differing from, for example, books in that they require 'non-trivial effort to traverse'" (Enevold & Hagstrom, 2009, p. 3). Ergodic media require effort beyond simply turning a page while scanning the text on paper or screen to progress the story or experience. Aarseth called games "'cybertexts', discarding the loose and general term 'interactive' privileging the more specific 'ergodic' to characterize the specific nature of games, MUDs, hypertexts etc. (Aarseth, 1997). In short, games should first and foremost be studied as games" (Enevold & Hagstrom, 2009, p. 3).

A MUD (multi-user dungeon) is a role-playing, text-based virtual realm. Hypertext is simply text on a computer screen that links to other text. Hypertext fictions are forms of electronic literature that challenge conceptions of text, author, and reader.[8] *Interactive* is still the dominant adjective applied to the medium, and I use it in this book because it is the most immediately understandable reminder of the element that sets

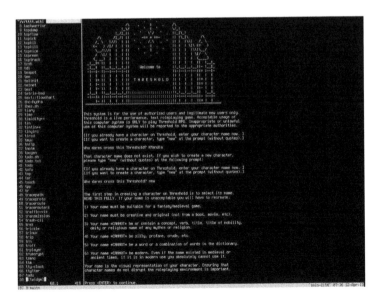

Figure 2.2 Screenshot of a MUD. Threshold [Video game]. (1996). Lexington, KY: Frogdice, Inc.

video game experiences apart from other acts of literacy and electracy. However, the specificity of the term ergodic should be understood as the critical aspect of interactivity. The use of the words *play* and *game* are applicable beyond video games as well and can be applied to cultural shifts and socially situated play experiences. Play theory incorporates this broader social definition, embracing the complexity of these terms and the nuanced means in which they implicate almost all elements of human experience.

The potential for a "breach in hegemony of the dominant" in ways that are consistent with that same hegemonic structure exists in professional sports, battles for popularity in high school cliques, and video games, just as it does in international or civil wars (Sutton-Smith, 2001, p. 98). In every interaction, we all *play the game*—communicate, understand, and act—according to the social rule-based system in which we were raised and according to the limitations of our current knowledge. It is important to keep this scaling level of meaning in mind when discussing play. For the purposes of this book, especially given its focus on the individual (ergodic ontogeny) rather than larger cultural shifts (ludic identity), the literal interpretation of the word *game* is most relevant.

2.2 Defining the Player

We must begin by exploring the relationship between media and audiences, attending "to both media and audience text uses in order to understand readers' multiplicitous and contextualized identities formed within the production and consumption of popular culture" (Hagood, 2008, p. 541). Hagood (2008) described media audiences, players of interactive digital games/ergodic cybertexts, as having "temporary, hybrid identities that shift and change by context" (p. 541). This active process of meaning-making takes place every day. We overhear some bit of information on a television screen in the corner of a restaurant, glance at a magazine cover while walking past a convenience store, or notice a headline in an online pop-up while signing in to our email. Each new piece of cultural data influences our understanding of the world at any given moment and moreover influences our sense of self in relation to this worldview. Attention should especially be paid to daily activities that are framed in terms of entertainment or play, which are potentially addressed with a less critical eye. To understand media influences, we must determine who experiences these media effects and define the audience/player.

Hypermedia, cybertexts, and other interactive forms are *used* by those who engage them. The adoptions of the term *use* for these media "also points to a potential problem with research in this area: do attempts to accommodate the complexity of the digital artifact by devising terms that synthesize the range of literacy processes involved in human-computer interaction deter us from attending to the distinctiveness of those processes" (Dobson, 2007, p. 266)? In other words, is it descriptive enough to deem the actor (one who performs the physical and mental processes necessary to create play) in gaming a *player* or simply a *user* of technology? The term *player* is used predominantly, with *user* or *agent* referring to interactive instances outside the realm of *game*, in this book but should not be considered a simplifying or neglectful term. To play through an ergodic text, one must engage multiple senses while relying on layered details of cultural and technical understanding and an acute awareness of the programming inherent to a given game.

Dobson (2007)[9] explained that, in a sense, readers were always "'players', because they necessarily reconstruct texts within their own worldviews by reading themselves into narratives, drawing inferences in order to fill in temporal, spatial or causal gaps, and ...hypermedia...must engage in an activity of construction and reconstruction," ultimately resulting in the coining of the term "wreading" (267).[10] The physical (visuals, audio, haptic feedback) and emotional connection of the player to the game world is crucial to understanding interactivity. Bogost (2011) explained that to "simulate the behavior, rather than just the appearance of texture, games have to use more than visual effects. Sound design is one answer...[and] simulated properties of the physical world can also contribute to texture" such as traction, gravity, and movement across different surfaces (p. 79). The video in Figure 2.3 demonstrates how sound design and physics create more realistic play experiences.

Figure 2.3 Immersion with QR Code. FIFA 17 [Video game]. (2016). Redwood City, CA: Electronic Arts. https://vimeo.com/185102472.

Haptic feedback is another technique employed by game designers; it is also called *rumble* due to its introduction to most players through use of the Nintendo 64 Rumble-Pack. Initial advertising for rumble-packs exaggerated the level of immersion through the inclusion of an un-required VR-visor type apparatus on the player to demonstrate (through hyperbole) the increased level of player sensation resulting from the new form of physical feedback. The haptic feedback of the rumble-pack is the movement in the physical game controller that correlates to actions viewed on screen. "In general, the use of rumble is of two kinds: the first is increased immersion...the second is better feedback...[to help] the player orient toward interface or gameplay goals" (Bogost, 2011, p. 80–81). Through the myriad of sensory perceptions now available to players, especially since the implementation of movement response with accessories for consoles like the Kinect or motion sensors on the Wii remote, player identification and interactivity reach new heights.

Games are not exclusively geared toward high levels of energy exertion, autonomic arousal, or even agitation. Arguably most gameplay experiences are relaxing for the player, leaning back and only physically moving fingers to navigate the terrain of the virtual world. Wii games, Kinect, and *Dance Dance Revolution* (1999–2016) titles are obvious exceptions. "Because relaxation and meditation rely on inaction rather than action, they threaten to undermine the very nature of video games. There's a fine line between producing Zen and satirizing it" (Bogost, 2011, p. 95). Some games' attempts at realism revert to mundane aspects of everyday life, like having a job. In *Shenmue* (1999), the main character must move a number of crates with a forklift as part of his day job.

Figure 2.4 Screenshot of *Shenmue.* Shenmue [Video game]. (1999). Tokyo, Japan: Sega.

Relaxation is possible in casual games or games with a slow, at times plodding, but overall satisfying pace, such as *Shenmue* (1999) or *Ico* (2002), during which rapid progression of the plot is not a requirement and not always incentivized. Exploration and enjoyment of character interactions replace action-based play.

The goal of most game designers is to create games that support habituation of players, games that are "easy to learn and hard to master": the formula that "purports to hold the key to a powerful outcome: an addicting game...in which starting is smooth and easy," also called Bushnell's Law after the founder of Atari who stated that "all the best games are easy to learn and difficult to master. They should reward the first quarter and the hundredth" (Bogost, 2011, p. 125). The allure of difficult mastery of games is that not *just anyone* can experience the game's entirety. Difficult games such as *Metal Gear Solid* (1998) or *Ninja Gaiden* (2004) can be *catchy*, a term Bogost uses in place of *addicting*, supporting the idea that replayable aspects of video games are more akin to the replayable parts of a pop song than to concepts traditionally related to addiction that have negative connotations.

2.3 Interactivity

The critical difference between past media and the digital media of computer/video games is the necessary action of the player, interactivity. Interactive narratives and gameplay do not exist without a player. More than simply words on a page not being read, the actual existence of the game cannot occur without a player. In the early years of virtual simulation, Barton (1972) suggested that traditionally neglected qualitative judgments be included in research on human-computer interaction. In Barton's research, game administrators observed behaviors in human players that were far more nuanced than the limited technological abilities of computers at the time. Barton's goal was to supplement verisimilitude (the reflection of reality, even if crude, for effective educational gaming) with additional criteria for effective game design. Human-computer interaction through simulation requires more than realistic graphical representations of reality to achieve a connection with the player. The inclusion and valuing of the player in research is critical to understanding the far more complex simulations of modern gaming consoles found in many homes today.

Aarseth's groundbreaking *Cybertext: Perspectives on Ergodic Literature* (1997) moved the discussion of player and computer game to a level of individual analysis beyond and external to other media forms. Aarseth's text outlined the differences between traditional literature and ergodic, which requires non-trivial effort to traverse the text in whatever form it may be. Though we may look at interactive digital narratives in a way that is similar to traditional literature such as books, plays, and even films, these are all distinctly different in that none make the reader/watcher/experiencing person acutely aware of a path not taken. As Aarseth (1997) pointed out, "when you read from a cybertext, you are constantly reminded of inaccessible strategies...each decision will make some parts of the text more, and others less, accessible, and you may never know the exact results of your choices; that is, exactly what you missed" (p. 3). The digital medium is interpreted and misinterpreted by literary theorists who rely on limited conceptions of computer programs, interactivity, hypertext, automated poetics, multiuser discourse, and adventure games. Each of these has some element, or in some cases multiple characteristics, in common with traditional literary media. Yet, the critical inclusion of the player to access, and also simultaneously neglect, parts of the text is missing, thus setting ergodic cybertexts apart.

In *Fable II* (2008), the main character proceeds along a path that could just as easily be postponed to another time or ignored altogether during game play. Non-linear texts can vary and produce different outcomes but are not wholly separate from the more dominant linear form. They must therefore be seen simply as "one of many thematizations of textual behavior: writing, literacy, inscription, and so on" (Aarseth, 1997, p. 42). This seemingly broad application of non-linearity must be both specified and heightened to account for the particular ways in which players navigate interactive digital gaming environments and stories. Aarseth argued that many definitions of interactivity are reduced to more accurately describing *participation*, or even more broadly *use*. These descriptions of forms of play are not incorrect but do not sufficiently account for the level of agency involved in narrative progression in this sense.

Figure 2.5 Screenshot of *Fable II*. Fable II [Video game]. (2008). Guildford, UK: Lionhead Studios.

Michael Joyce's *afternoon* (1990), an early hypertext fiction,[11] provides insight into the nature of the term ergodics, as opposed to narration, and the ways in which it can be applied to extremely non-traditional texts such as narratives experienced via interactive progression through a visual, digital environment with oral and written cues. Aarseth (1997) supported the idea that there are narrative elements in *afternoon* but posited that there is also an "opposite force, a destabilizing disfiguration that bears down on the reader's patience and sense of progress. To counter this anti-hermeneutic circle, the reader has to become a metareader, mapping the network and reading the map of her own reading carefully" (p. 93). This in itself is not interactivity but is a "strategic counterattack upon the limited role or perspective offered to the reader by the hermetic text and an effort to regain a sense of readership" (Aarseth, 1997, p. 94). The idea of collaborative authorship in gaming is not entirely accurate either as the available code, though extensive, is still finite.

Early adventure games, and all early video games due to technical, time, and funding limitations, were of comparatively low *literary quality* (Buckles, 1985). The tendency to categorize games as non-literary, or unworthy of rigorous academic study, remains a stigma to a certain extent despite drastic leaps in narrative structure and the importance of story in digital gameplay. New media literacy and electronic literature studies are rapidly growing fields of inquiry that inform game studies and interactive entertainment media research. Aarseth (1997) took umbrage with the term *story,* as used by Buckles (1985) in relation to adventure games, and suggested that it lacks the necessary concepts of strangeness, as posited by Viktor Shklovskij and "leerstellen – blanks, gaps" (p. 110). The players of ergodic texts fill in the semantic gaps to complete the literary work but are also not authors themselves; they are something in between.

A video game is a cultural object with a specific historical context, but the gaps to which Aarseth alluded are an integral part of its materiality. As Galloway (2006) described, the object or artifact is *incomplete* in itself, and "without action, games remain only in the pages of an abstract rule book...video games come into being when the machine is powered up and the software is executed; they exist when enacted" (p. 2). Galloway (2006) suggested that one "should resist equating gamic action with a theory of 'interactivity' or the 'active audience' theory of media" which claim that audiences bring their own interpretations to media, and embraced the claim that an "active medium is one whose very materiality moves and restructures itself – pixels turning on and off, bits shifting in hardware registers, disks spinning up and spinning down...and prefer[s] instead to call the video game, like the computer, an action-based medium" (p. 3). This description is apt, though the term *interactivity,* if applied clearly in reference to ergodic

Figure 2.6 Screenshot of *Rage*. Rage [Video game]. (2011). Mesquite, TX: id
Software.

texts as distinguished from other media, is still arguably accurate in its
description. Action is not only partaken by the player but exists in the ebb
and flow of information/input between computer and the person playing.
Action is a key component of the unique qualities of this medium.

Load times and disc noises are rarely distracting (and are minimized
with each new iteration of gaming technology), because players recognize
the technological component of their virtual experiences. Figure 2.6
demonstrates instances of noticeable hardware effects, in this case texture pop-in as the game loads.

Geertz's (1972) concept of *deep play* positions culture as a document,
more specifically an *acted* document. Galloway (2006) argued that
"with literature or cinema there are important connections to the action of the author...but as texts they are not action-based in the same
sense that culture is and...video games are" (p. 14). Similar to Geertz's
description of the Balinese Cockfight,[12] if play is "a symbolic action
for larger issues in culture" then "video games render social realities
into playable form" (Galloway, 2006, p. 17). The process and experience
of play *is* this action in all its forms, be it puzzle solving, finding safe
paths of retreat for a non-player character to follow, shooting at enemies,
methodically building up points through repetitive tasks, or any other
possibility. Whether representative of culture on a more sophisticated
level than past media or not, interactive play in the form of console and
computer games can certainly engage the (w)reader/player in unique
ways that merit complex consideration.

2.4 Evoking Human-Computer Interaction

Interactive media and video game research must not confound theories of realism (based on realistic representation) with those that focus on actual extensions of real life (training simulators, for example).[13] The connection to action is that "games are an active medium that requires constant physical input by the gamer: action, doing, pressing buttons, controlling, and...because of this, a realist game must be realist in doing, in action" (Galloway, 2006, p. 8). The gamer is not simply an audience member, but an active participant/creator of play. However, the player is also limited by the program and design present. Therefore, any analysis of players can only be of the act of doing/using the game, which ties the gamer directly to his/her experience of the game.

Similarly, the mode and depth of interactivity that are possible in a given game have an effect on game narrative options (Page & Thomas, 2011). Galloway (2006) argued that computer games "signal a third phase for realism. The first two phases were realism in narrative (literature) and realism in images (painting, photography, film). Now there is also realism in action" (p. 9). Gamers do not merely view the medium as they experience it, they perform it. Realism in games must rely on more than accurate visual representations and create meaningful correspondences with realities in the physical and social world of players outside the game space.

This point begs the question of whether social interaction is possible between human beings and computers. Some claims made about human-computer interaction (HCI) suggest that people react socially to computers as though they were people, which prompted experiments on how interactions with computers are different from interpersonal human interactions (Reeves & Nass, 1996). Interpersonal goals are the differentiating factor between interactions with humans and computers, but what are the goals of interacting with a video game? The interactive nature of narrative progression in console or computer games does much more than provide a computer-mediated means of conversation. There are explicit goals inherent to gameplay bound within the rules and spaces of the virtual world created by the game's designers and programmers.

Bogost (2011) provided an overview of trends in video game analysis, simplifying the nuanced argumentation of Aarseth, Galloway, and others. Bogost (2011) acknowledged the necessity of looking at both form and function and argued that "the medium is the message, but the message is the message, too," suggesting that rather than "ignoring it, we ought to explore the relationships between the general properties of a medium and the particular situations in which it is used" (p. 5). Moving through video game space is a "strange way to get a sense of the space between two points when one could simply find a local park or just go outside and walk around the neighborhood," especially considering common accusations that video games are "ripping people out of the natural world and placing them into an artificial one. But this objection misses an important feature...the necessary unfamiliarity of a space being traversed" (Bogost, 2011, p. 50). Interactivity, in conjunction with movement through the virtual space itself, makes up the gameplay experience. Through our actions within the virtual realm, provided by computer-mediated experience, we may traverse unknown landscapes and expect interactions that would be wholly impossible in our reality-based physical circumstances, whether socially, economically, or geographically.

Wardrip-Fruin[14] (2007) investigated the function of story in role-playing games (RPGs) and playable media and argued that adventure (narrative-driven) games are still limited in the levels of agency, in this case meaning *freedom of action*, that they can provide for players. Digital RPGs offer "a richer character design and inventory system... and quite often there is a choice of which path to take next, reducing the degree of linearity" (Wardrip-Fruin, 2007, p. 9). However, this type of game is still strongly tied to a story that eventually progresses along the same lines for any given player despite moments of increased freedom of choice in the short term. Digital RPGs run the risk of limited replay value due to the linearity of a single story that dictates overall gameplay.

The complexity of real-time digital RPGs developed quickly in recent years. Character choices now lead to detailed narratives along divergent paths depending on decisions made by the player at certain points. This potential will be discussed in more detail regarding the use of character personalization, dialogue trees, and morality scales in the next chapters. Wardrip-Fruin (2007) posited that the "indie RPG movement takes as its guidepost what they call 'Gamist-Narrativist-Simulationist theory,' which holds that role-playing gamers seek traditional game play experiences, excellent stories, or some form of realism" (p. 11) but does not include the idea of moral or personal character development that emerged in recent years. Interactive digital games create an audience experience in "combination with the efforts of a group of human players," an experience that is constructed by players as well as by game design, interaction, and procedure, and these games "demand we be prepared to consider them for their characters, fictional worlds, use of language, and so on" (Wardrip-Fruin, 2007, p. 108). Stuart Moulthrop's *Pax* (2003) is self-described as "a 'textual instrument,' [that] specifically points us toward an aesthetics of playing that isn't game-centric" but player-centric (Wardrip-Fruin, 2007, p. 108).

Play has more meaning and influence than simple entertainment value, though the pleasure of play must not be forgotten. Some game makers use play as a window into real-world political and social development or activism. In John Tynes' chapter "Prismatic Play," he argued that the development of "engagist works" embrace the "modern world around us instead of rejecting it for a fantastic otherworld" (Wardrip-Fruin, 2007, p. 221). Bogost's *Persuasive Games*[15] design group is a prominent example.

Figure 2.7 Screenshot of *Pax*. Moulthrop, S. (2003). *Pax: An instrument.* Retrieved from https://elmcip.net/creative-work/pax-instrument.

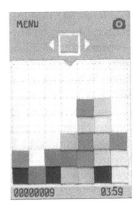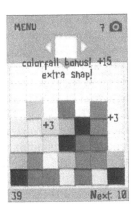

Figure 2.8 Screenshot of *Colorfall*. Colorfall [Video game]. (2010). Retrieved from http://persuasivegames.com/game/colorfall.

For instance, the game *Colorfall* (2010–2016) was created to promote physical activity while supporting cognitive health through basic mental challenges. Whether serious, educational, entertaining, escapist, or propagandistic, the ways in which game narrative influences human understanding beyond the game world is a crucial point of analysis in game studies.

The multiple locations of media convergence in everyday life require human subjects to be in a state of heightened media awareness at all times, navigating the nuanced variation between various remediations of electronic data. Increasingly, single consoles (beginning with the PlayStation 3) embody media convergence in their function as game console, Blu-Ray player, CD player, and Internet access point all-in-one. The current generation of consoles (Xbox One and PS4) exaggerate this convergence and attempt to exploit its potential even further.[16] It therefore becomes more difficult to separate game-playing hardware from other new media technology. As Griffiths and Light[17] (2008) explained, certain ideological underpinnings shift once media convergence reaches this point of compilation. They utilized the ideas of Social Shaping of Technology Theory (SST) "based upon a critique of social and technological determinism" (Griffiths & Light, 2008, p. 451) to support a moral disconnect between interactions in the game world and the non-game world. Players' ethical values shift depending on contextual factors. This point is confirmed through analysis of the interview data collected in this book as well. Classification is important because "social networking includes gaming and gaming includes social networking; this evolution further blurs ethical considerations as social networking might normally be associated with 'reality' and digital gaming with 'fantasy'" (Griffiths & Light, 2008, p. 457). The game world may increase a sense of anonymity and a lessened sense of reality for some players.[18]

Ideological shifts may manifest in online interaction, online games, digital interactive narratives, or some combination of each.[19] The concept of ergodic ontogeny presented in this book counters the idea of a necessary ignorance of real-world impact by gamers and must certainly acknowledge that players know they are playing, know the limitations of hardware and the Internet's reach, and may alter their personas in ways that exploit this knowledge. The study of ergodic ontogeny reorients the field of interactive media studies to be subject-driven while valuing programming choices and technical potential, expanding and reworking definitions of literacy and text. Understanding the complex ways in which players influence and are influenced by interactive media, and the interactions that take place during gameplay, is an ongoing task.

The objectives of this book are similar to the concept of *phantasmal media* posited by Harrell (2013), which explored the experience of semiotic cues and personal archetypes that create meaning for individuals, and suggested ways that interactive media should be designed to empower rather than oppress. Ergodic ontogeny is less experiential; it is an interdisciplinary approach to reflection on a developmental process over time as individuals create and solidify their senses of self. Ergodic ontogeny combines internal and external influences on personal experience, expression, and agentive play to address cultural shifts in key elements of identity such as gender-identification, culturally situated hierarchies and social capital, and consciousness of media influence.

The conceptual underpinnings of remediation and premediation that Grusin (2010) suggested are foundational components of media experience in modern times. The concept of ergodic ontogeny builds on concepts established by Shaviro (2010),[20] Calleja (2011), and others[21] to reintegrate post-cinematic affect and experiences of player involvement and immersion into individuals' processes of identity construction that influence choices within and beyond gameplay or digital involvement. Predefined disciplinary concepts of *literacy* and *media affect* lack cohesive and comprehensive terms for talking about some aspects of media use that are unique to interactive digital play. Detailed discussions of the limitations of literacy as a term and ways it may be altered to maintain relevance are essential as narratives forms shift quickly along with new technological capabilities. The idea that we are shifting to entirely mediated signification alters, and to some extent negates, prior systems of representation, organizing signification through the *hyperreal* (pre/re) mediation of a screen, a concept that will be returned to in later chapters.

McGonigal (2011) helped set the stage for why games matter and how they can be used to solve real-world problems,[22] a premise that supports the concept of ergodic ontogeny and establishes the real-world need to understand the relationship between games and players. Our modes of analysis and basic language structure are situated within culturally and historically specific experiences. Harrell's (2013) use of the term phantasmal media, for instance, "refers to the ways that computational media can be used for the subjective, cultural, and critical aims of prompting humans to generate both individual and shared combinations of sensory imaginative impressions and ideology" (p. 22). A constant process of remaking language (and all semiotic forms) is essential and moves beyond traditional concepts of text- or screen-based *literacy* and requires new levels of complexity be applied to the concept of *play*. As an active agent in the narrative structure, the moral and psychological components of games exist as a reflection of the player. I am interested in long-term individual effects on identity development and how these affective shifts manifest—the process of ergodic ontogeny.

The computer-mediated discourse of video game *texts* is multidimensional and has the potential to blur the line between the virtual and the real. The next chapters incorporate sociolinguistic analyses of interview data from which themes emerge to spur discussions of identity, ethics/morality, and cultural stereotypes. These analyses detail the ways in which individuals experience ergodic ontogeny in their own terms and describe trends reflected in modern interactive digital texts and game studies theories.

Notes

1 Sutton-Smith's *The Ambiguity of Play* (2001) traced the history of play theory along its winding path toward modernity, post-modernity, and beyond and is a good overview/starting point for readers in this field.
2 The signals referenced by Bateson denote traditional semiotic terms, not the additional layer of the virtual.
3 Sutton-Smith (2001) separated the concept of play into specific categories including mind/subjective play, solitary play, playful behaviors, informal

social play, vicarious audience play, performance play, celebrations and festivals, contests (games/sports), and risky or deep play. Beyond the diversity of forms of play, there are also diverse players—all ages, genders, groupings—with differences in play agencies and scenarios (even playful scholars).

4 See Boocock and Schild (1968).

5 This, however, seems to indicate that the purpose of play, as it is experienced by players in the moment, is merely that of immediate and temporary enjoyment. Sutton-Smith (2001) cautioned that play is a complex developmental form in itself with scaling levels moving between the inability to play as pathology, play as a form of security, as stereotypic, and playful forms of play. Social understandings of these forms are developed as children become more familiar with the nuanced uses and expressions of play in their particular culture.

6 For example, if one loses as part of a team, "one's own group frequently develops a desire to contest [the superiority of the victors]...This opposition is a...breach in the hegemony of the dominant groups, even though the playing of the same games is itself consistent with such hegemony" (Sutton-Smith, 2001, p. 98).

7 Variations on this system of power structures and its related gaming activities can be understood in terms of direct ludic identity (taking on the imperial sports structure), contestive ludic identity (fighting the dominant group), and counter-ludic identity (when a conquered group puts more emphasis on its own folk games). Other concepts include inversive ludic identities in which a local group is introduced to dominant play, but "transforms it, so it becomes an upside-down synthesis with its own preexisting forms," similar to usurpative ludic identity in which those in power usurp control over local activities to extend their control (Sutton-Smith, 2001, p. 100).

8 For information about Moulthrop's *Victory Garden* hypertext, visit http://www.eastgate.com/catalog/VictoryGarden.html.

9 Dobson conducted a three-year study with readers and writers of computer-based texts with non-linear narrative structures. Reading and writing, being given information as opposed to constructing knowledge, are distinct experiences. Further contextualization is necessary to achieve true digital literacy (Dobson, 2007; Dovey & Kennedy 2006).

10 This term is meant to convey a metaphor of reading as an act of writing, similar to "Barthes' notion of lisible and scriptable texts [which] tends in this direction (Barthes, 1974), as does the Derridean doctrine of écriture (Derrida, 1976)" (Dobson, 2007, p. 267). However, Derrida (1981) also specified that reading as a form of writing is an incomplete description, and we must first determine what kind of writing reading actually is; the risk of conflating these two terms is a phenomenological concern.

11 This is considered the first hypertext. To see a brief video demonstration of *afternoon* (1989), visit http://www.youtube.com/watch?v=djIrHF8S6-Q.

12 In his essay "Deep Play: Notes on the Balinese Cockfight" (1972), Geertz described cockfighting in Bali as a *representation of* and *creator of* culture.

13 An additional layer of complexity arises in the realization that play has its own sense of reality.

14 *First Person: New Media as Story, Performance and Game* (Wardrip-Fruin & Harrington, 2006) acted as a catalyst for Wardrip-Fruin's book, *Second Person* (2007), which investigated the function of story in role-playing (RPGs) and playable media.

15 To explore their games online, visit http://www.persuasivegames.com/games/.

16 The Xbox One's initial release, for example, was criticized for some aspects of such convergence due to requirements that the system have a consistent Internet connection (limiting use by those whose socioeconomic conditions might prohibit such access) and the tying of data to an individual so that games could not be shared. For an overview, visit Forbes.com at http://www.forbes.com/sites/erikkain/2013/05/27/the-five-biggest-problems-with-the-xbox-one/#73482c0a42ce.

17 Griffiths and Light (2008) explored the "basic features of ethics—a concern with interpretations of morality—and developing an understanding of the ethical issues that arise in the context of the convergence where media components have previously been classified in different ways" (p. 448).

18 In Griffith and Light's (2008) research, respondents justified and rationalized intentionally scamming other players/members of online gaming communities.

19 Blizzard Entertainment, makers of *World of Warcraft,* closed their Auction House for a time due to hacker crime (http://eu.battle.net/wow/en/blog/10310774/Account_Security_Warning-25_06_2013). Gold farming, a process through which people in the real world spend time in-game and sell items for real money to players with less free time, was a growing concern. Griefing or harassing other players by acting outside agreed upon norms, especially in MMORPGs, is a similar issue.

20 Shaviro (2010) grappled with the affective process as a result of new media, specifically after 9/11.

21 See also Malaby's *Making Virtual Worlds* (2009), Taylor's *Play Between Worlds* (2006), Pearce and Artemesia's *Communities of Play* (2009), and Yee's *The Proteus Paradox* (2014).

22 Madigan (2015) addressed the psychology of video game play but not interdisciplinary approaches to cultural theory beyond the strictly psychological perspective.

References

Aarseth, E. J. (1997). *Cybertext: Perspectives on ergodic literature.* Baltimore, MD: Johns Hopkins University Press.

Barton, R. F. (1972). Incorporating qualitative judgments into man-computer simulations. *Simulation and Games, 3*(1), 79–88.

Bateson, G. (1955). A theory of play and phantasy. *Psychiatric Research Reports, 2*, 39–51.

Bogost, I. (2011). *How to do things with video games.* Minneapolis, MN: University of Minnesota Press.

Boocock, S., & Schild, E. (1968). *Stimulation games in learning.* Thousand Oaks, CA: Sage Publications.

Buckles, M. (1985). Interactive fiction: The computer storygame "Adventure." San Diego, CA: University of California Press.

Calleja, G. (2011). *In-game: From immersion to incorporation.* Cambridge, MA: The MIT Press.

Derrida, J. (1981). *Dissemination.* Chicago, IL: University of Chicago Press.

Dobson, T. M. (2007). In medias res: Reading, writing, and the digital artefact. *E-Learning, 4*(3), 266–272.

Dovey, J., & Kennedy, H. (2006). *Game cultures: Computer games as new media*. Maidenhead, UK: Open University Press.

Enevold, J., & Hagström, C. (2009). Mothers, play and everyday life: Ethnology meets game studies. *Ethnologia Scandinavica, 39*, 27–41.

Fagen, R. (1981). *Animal play behavior*. New York, NY: Oxford University Press.

Galloway, A. R. (2006). *Gaming: Essays on algorithmic* culture. Minneapolis, MN: University of Minnesota Press.

Geertz, C. (1972). Deep play: Notes on the Balinese cockfight. *Daedalus, 101*(1), 1–37.

Griffiths, M., & Light, B. (2008). Social networking and digital gaming media convergence: Classification and its consequences for appropriation. *Information Systems Frontiers, 10*(4), 447–459.

Grusin, R. (2010). *Premediation: Affect and mediality after 9/11*. New York, NY: Palgrave Macmillan.

Hagood, M. C. (2008). Intersections of popular culture, identities, and new literacies research. In J. Coiro, M. Knobel, C. Lankshear, & D. Leu (Eds.), *Handbook of research on new literacies* (p. 531–551). New York, NY: Taylor & Francis.

Harrell, D. F. (2013). *Phantasmal media: An approach to imagination, computation, and expression*. Cambridge, MA: The MIT Press.

Joyce, M. (1990). *Afternoon: A story*. Watertown, MA: Eastgate Systems.

Madigan, J. (2015). Getting gamers: The psychology of video games and their impact on the people who play them. Lanham, MD: Rowman & Littlefield.

Malaby, T. (2009). *Making virtual worlds: Linden lab and Second Life*. Ithaca, NY: Cornell University Press.

McGonigal, J. (2011). Reality is broken: Why games make us better and how they can change the world. New York, NY: The Penguin Press.

Moulthrop, S. (2003). *Pax: An instrument*. Retrieved from https://elmcip.net/creative-work/pax-Instrument.

Newman, J. (2004). *Difficult questions about video games*. Nottingham, U.K.: Suppose Partners.

Page, R., & Thomas, B. (2011). *New narratives: Stories and storytelling in the digital age*. Lincoln, NE: University of Nebraska Press.

Pearce, C. & Artemesia. (2009). *Communities of play: Emergent cultures in multiplayer games and virtual worlds*. Cambridge, MA: The MIT Press.

Reeves, B., & Nass, C. (1996). *The media equation: How people treat computers, television, and new media like real people and places*. Stanford, CA: CSLI Publications.

Shaviro, S. (2010). *Post-cinematic affect*. Winchester, UK: Zero Books.

Sutton-Smith, B. (2001). *The ambiguity of play*. Cambridge, MA: Harvard University Press.

Taylor, T. L. (2006). *Play between worlds: Exploring online game culture*. Cambridge, MA: The MIT Press.

Wardrip-Fruin, N. (2007). *Second person: Role-playing and story in games and playable media*. Cambridge, MA: MIT Press.

Wardrip-Fruin, N., & Harrigan, P. (Eds.). (2006). *First person: New media as story, performance, and game*. Cambridge, MA: MIT Press.

Yee, N. (2014). *The proteus paradox: How online games and virtual worlds change us – and how they don't*. New Haven, CT: Yale University Press.

3   Human-Computer Interaction

I mean, there was an eyeball in his lap, and just seeing that in real life. And smelling it in real life. It was still very shocking for me. And do I feel like games desensitized it for me? No...No.

—George

This chapter includes current conceptions of the language of new media, the complexity of a sociolinguistic analysis of people's talk about game experiences, and interview data. Interview analysis involves reporting what was said, analyzing how it was said, and positing potential meanings in sociocultural terms while keeping in mind the fact that this writing is itself a form of discourse that must be critically examined just as is the work of the theorists described in the initial sections of this chapter. It is important to stress that the information presented here is but a single iteration of these themes though many interpretations are possible. Not all players experience games and play in the same way. What is crucial, however, is to investigate the multiple ways in which conceptions of self in reality are formed through interactive virtual experiences of play—the ways in which ergodic ontogeny is experienced, expressed, and best understood. Clarification of this concept requires detailed background information about the various disciplines that inform interactive media research as well as tangible examples provided by game players themselves.

3.1 Game Literacy and Representation: Remediation, Immediacy, and Language

Building on play theory, the study of *game literacy* references elements of computer-mediated interactivity and its relation to new media discourses of play. Communicative forms are ever increasing,[1] with signs bombarding us at every turn, yet the very proliferation of these symbols lends to their conscious transparency.[2] The influence of media is still felt, but we notice less the mass input of modern society due to its constant inescapable presence. This leads to complicated questions about the influence of new media and digital interactivity in instances of media convergence[3] such as online play or computer games with multimodal narrative structures. If experiences within or via a medium are indiscernible from experiences in life outside the influence of that media (should that exist in modern societies at all), then how can we differentiate (or grapple with the overlapping qualities of) our sense of self and understandings of the world around us in ways that are determinably pre- or post-media influence?

Graphical user interfaces (GUI), similar to digital graphics in film, for example, are meant to be forms of transparent immediacy (though film usually utilizes non-immersive digital graphics, non-VR). Digital graphics are meant to blend seamlessly with the film or video of actors and physical sets to create the desired effect. GUI's, of course, operate solely for this purpose. Their "immediacy is supposed to make [a] computer interface 'natural' rather than arbitrary" (Bolter & Grusin, 2000, p. 23). The immediacy of computer games exists through interactivity: "the fact that these media can change their point of view in response to the viewer or user" (Bolter & Grusin, 2000, p. 81). This interactivity may be exhibited through hypermediacy:[4] an awareness of the medium and acceptance of an imperfect visual recreation. Computer games in particular display this form of hypermediacy in that some developers demonstrate little if any concern with media transparency while others make explicit use of first-person POV subjectivities.

Game designers utilize different perspectives to engage players and visually represent their gamic actions on screen, for example, third-person and first-person points of view.

Figure 3.1 Player POV. Star Wars: Battlefront [Video game]. (2015). Redwood City, CA: Electronic Arts.

Bolter and Grusin (2000) categorized games as remediations of the computer but also of television and film as they are played on repurposed screens.[5] Remediation is relevant because players bring expectations of other/past media to their experiences of digital interactive gaming.[6] The video in Figure 3.2 includes cinematic game play incorporating visuals akin to the expectations of film viewership such as lens flair, exaggerated fight scenes, and dialogue.

However, it is increasingly common for computer monitors and television screens to be purchased with gaming in mind as a primary function (purposed, not re-purposed). The Wii U, Nintendo Switch, and other consoles with screens built into their controllers bring new layers of play potential and multimodal interactions of remediation that can occur simultaneously during games or simply while interacting with the system's user interface.

The ways in which players, as well as those analyzing play, talk about interactive digital media necessarily change the outcome of analyses. Manovich (2002) provided a detailed exploration of language in new media and suggested that modern visual culture is related to avant-garde film. "A hundred years after cinema's birth, cinematic ways of seeing the world, of structuring time, of narrating a story, of linking one experience to the next, have become the basic means by which computer users access and interact with cultural data" (Manovich, 2002, p. xv). Manovich argued that the "computerization of culture not only leads to the emergence of new cultural forms such as computer games and virtual worlds; it redefines existing ones" (p. 9).[7] The way we view the world is dependent on our conceptions of reality that are necessarily based in relationships to cultural texts like video games, film, television, literature, cultural traditions, folk tales, and so on. People living in societies with a different set of cultural input will experience the world

Figure 3.2 Cinematic game play with QR Code. Star Wars: Battlefront [Video game]. (2015). Redwood City, CA: Electronic Arts. https://vimeo.com/185081165.

in a different way. This seems obvious but warrants discussion due to the ubiquitous nature of mass media. New media combines the potentials of past media to create newly emergent forms but also changes our expectations of and ways of using older forms of media.[8] Games' connection to film is strengthened in that computer games incorporate cinematic interfaces by featuring detailed sequences that alternate between interactive segments requiring player action and non-interactive cut scenes. Increasingly, the cinematic quality of storytelling is built directly into playable game moments.

The remediation of film literacy into games is a reflection of the innate influential power of forms of media communication. The similarities between films and video games are often quite obvious. There are some games that reference game tradition itself (self-referential, retro, or nostalgic elements of games) rather than film tradition. Examples of games that make explicit mention or design use of looking *like a video game* include titles such as *Hotline Miami* (2012), *Meat Boy* (2008), and *3D Dot Game Heroes* (2009). Game makers expect to reach the largest audiences and yield the greatest commercial and financial successes by playing by the rules of past media. The concept of the *screen* is important in remediation, but it changes with simulation. The "simulation tradition aims to blend virtual and physical spaces rather than to separate them...their boundary is de-emphasized (rather than being marked by a rectangular frame, as in the representation tradition); the spectator is free to move around the physical space" (Manovich, 2002, p. 112). Interactive digital media do less to represent reality within the confines of a screen, a concept closer to an image in a painting, and more to draw the player in to a new (virtual) reality that is not confined.

This point has some distinguishing characteristics from Bolter and Grusin's argument, which stated that hypermediacy is equally prevalent in all media. For Manovich, virtual reality (VR) is empty space. Games like *Shadow of the Colossus* (2005, 2011) and *Skyrim* (2013) have vast open, traversable spaces. Virtual reality can be moved through, not simply seen.

Through interactive movement in a game world, "we are one step away from VR, where physical space is totally disregarded, and all 'real actions' take place in virtual space," an experience described as a moment when the screen could disappear "because what was behind it simply took over" (Manovich, 2002, p. 114). Though we are not there yet, the dynamic, interactive nature of simulations certainly provides additional immersion far beyond the flat linear space of past media.

The idea that we are shifting to entirely mediated signification began perhaps most distinctly with Baudrillard's notion of simulation culture, or *the hyperreal*, which "interrogates the cultural forms of media communications" and described the ways in which "popular culture preempts the exchange of symbols between individuals, introducing another

Figure 3.3 Traversable space with QR Code. Grand Theft Auto V [Video game]. (2013). New York, NY: Take-Two Interactive. Red Dead Redemption [Video game]. (2010). New York, NY: Take-Two Interactive. https://vimeo.com/185105025.

layer of experience that undermines the subject's ability to define and to grasp the truth" (Poster, 2001, p. 121). Electronic mediation indelibly alters and to some extent negates prior systems of representation, detaching signs from their referents and organizing signification through the *hyperreal* mediation of a screen. There are certainly examples of retreats from hypermediacy, often viewed as vacations from modernity/real-life in which people *unplug* from daily routines, yet the predominant experience of modern society involves layers of digitally mediated cultural exchange on a moment-to-moment basis.

Kress (2000) provided another theory of media representation and suggested that theories of language cannot suffice; "the multimodal texts/messages of the era of multiliteracies need a theory which deals adequately with the processes of integration/composition of the various modes in these texts: both in production/making and in consumption/reading"[9] (p. 153). Our modes of analysis and basic language structure are situated within culturally and historically specific experiences. The way people express themselves is both a representation of the media influences that surround them and a force onto those media forms.[10] Understanding is limited in terms of the ideas, frames of reference, social narratives, words, and phrases that are available in our personal realities.

This constant process of remaking language (and all semiotic forms) is essential to expression; expression accounts for action and interaction within and between media. Kress and Van Leeuwen (2001) outlined a theory of interactive multimedia communication through detailed modes of semiotic, cultural, linguistic, and anthropological theory without ignoring the design and function of new media models.[11] Games take fuller advantage of and engage more senses than written language.

Figure 3.4 Screenshot of *In the Pit*. In the Pit [Video game]. (2009). Retrieved from http://www.studiohunty.com/itp/.

Kress' notion of remaking meaning through communicative forms fits nicely with video games' reliance on player input and individual experiences of game play. An interesting example of a game that relies on player's cultural knowledge of the language of video games, but focuses on only one sense, is *In the Pit* (Studio Hunty 2006), an Xbox Live indie title that uses no visual cues whatsoever.

3.2 Ergodic Literature and Computer-Mediated Communication

The term *text* has been used thus far to describe an object of analysis. A film, game, or other cultural artifact can be considered a *text* that can be *read* according to the appropriate understanding of literacy. Describing games as a form of literature relies on the metaphorical context of these terms, though literature also sometimes implies written words and narratives within an interactive digital game. Computer games are a unique environment for the use of text (in this case the literal letters and words in an order than can be read according to traditional understandings of writing and literacy) rather than a new textual genre entirely (Ryan, 1999, p. 8). In *Cyberspace Textuality* (1999), Aarseth contributed an additional angle of analysis to the concept of computer-based game literacy: an analysis of ergodic literature. As previously described, *ergodic* is a combination of words *work* and *path/road*, and "it is used to describe a type of discourse whose signs emerge as a path produced by a non-trivial element of work. Ergodic phenomena are produced by some kind of cybernetic system, i.e., a machine (or a human) that operates as an information feedback loop, which will generate a different semiotic sequence each time it is engaged" (Ryan, 1999, p. 32–33).

Generalizations about the aesthetics of ergodics are somewhat meaningless, necessitating reliance on case-by-case analyses of individual cultural artifacts or texts, but the categorization of these phenomena as dependent on a human-computer feedback loop is accurate and specific. It provides a means of understanding the ways in which each play experience is in many ways unique despite potential limitations of programming that may imply a uniform result. Aarseth explained that the "relationship between the narrative and the ergodic is dialectic, not dichotomic. Narrative structures and elements can be found in ergodic works, and narrative works may contain ergodic features" (Ryan, 1999, p. 34).

House of Leaves (Danielewski, 2000) is an example of a book (text-based in physical form) that incorporates ergodic elements (requiring non-trivial effort to traverse). It is essential to note the differences between the effort-inducing organization of text on a page and the virtual elements of interactive media in video games. Video games are not meant to be intentionally obfuscatory and on the contrary usually aim for Bushnell's Law of being easy to learn yet difficult to master. Interactive digital media is seamlessly ergodic (even when calling direct attention to its own ludic elements or commenting on games themselves) without the overt, and potentially jarring, effect that a text-based ergodic work evokes.

Computer games have only description, not narration, according to Aarseth, "since there is no such thing as the unfolding of a predetermined story. The ergodic level usually dominates the descriptive...while depending on the descriptive elements to concretize the path through the event space" (Ryan, 1999, p. 35). Once ergodic elements are fully realized, sequences are produced and narratively reproduced as a story. By this rationale, purely semiotic theories of computer-mediated phenomena generally fail because "they are not concerned with the sign-producing mechanism, without which the cybernetic sign processes cannot be properly understood" (Ryan, 1999, p. 36). Semiotic theory, therefore, is viewed as ill-equipped to properly describe ergodic discourses, which require their own terms and theorizations.

The *Mass Effect* series (2007–2017), real-time action role-playing games, provides well-known examples of characters beginning a game sequence under the limitations of narrative and advancing the story in different directions based on their input. The following video from IGN. com (https://www.youtube.com/watch?v=iHrFG4AXsMg) explains these capabilities and demonstrates the distinct outcomes of one section of *Mass Effect 3* (2012).

Discourses of interactive media play are dependent on human communication with technology. The study of non-linear discourse through computer-mediated communication (CMC) takes a closer look at academic discourse and at the particular media that are valued over others. This type of research helps to determine popular cultural trends in understanding new media forms—if games are, for instance, devalued academically then they may be devalued in broader social terms. Daisley (1994)[12] noted an early article on CMC in which "Marcia Halio was critiqued for her report of initial findings in a comparison of Macintosh and IBM users (1990a)" (p. 109).[13] "Critics...focused primarily on her methodology...[but] what no one...seemed to notice at the time was that her rhetoric itself seemed to be an indictment of

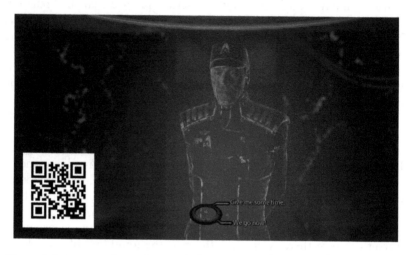

Figure 3.5 Integrated storyline with QR Code. Mass Effect 3 [Video game]. (2012). Edmonton, Canada: Bioware. www.youtube.com/watch?v= iHrFG4AXsMg.

play" (Daisley, 1994, p. 109). Whether her method was sound or not, the report was phrased in such ways that play,[14] regardless of application (scholarly or otherwise), was detrimental to learning processes.

The study of computer-mediated discourse (CMD) is a subset of CMC that focuses on language and language use analyzed through discourse analysis (Herring, 2001). Many researchers consider computer networks to be a distinct medium, different from writing or speaking. "Thus CMD researchers speak of electronic 'medium effects' on CMD, rather than treating CMD as a form of 'writing' (typing) that happens to be distributed by electronic means" (Herring, 2001, p. 2). Typing into a computer or interacting with data in a video game is not inherently a new kind of communication but *is* distinguished by the effects of the medium through which the communication takes place.

There are situational factors that influence CMD as well. "Different participation structures (Baym, 1996) such as one-to-one, one-to-many, or many-to-many; the distinction between public and private exchanges; and the degree of anonymity provided by the system all have potential consequences for language use" (Herring, 2001, p. 10). There are many modes of both synchronous and asynchronous communication in CMD that play important roles in new media studies as related to social gaming interactions. The interview data in this and the following chapters reflect these distinctions. Discourse with and about a computer or non-player character differs from discourse with or about other human players whether in the same room or across a networked virtual play environment.

The unique qualities of interactive digital gaming communication include both the ludic and narrative elements of play. These elements of discourse influence personal identity construction. As is the case with CMD, the medium through which discourse takes place necessarily effects the individual playing. Human identity is constructed through "expressions [that] not only mediate between us and our world (referentiality) and between us and our fellow man (communicability), but also between us and ourselves (self-understanding)," and changes in such mediation "reflect changes in the relationship between us and our world, in our social relationships, and in our self-conception" (Raessens & Goldstein, 2005, p. 251).[15] In order to be, games have to be played.[16] Juul (2011) contended that rule-based action is the predominant element of gaming in video game play and explored the idea that "video games are rules and fiction…in this instance the fiction, the sentiment of *as if* replaces and performs the same function as do rules. Rules themselves create fictions" (p. 12–13). The rules of a video game may be overtly stated as the player learns the goals and systems of play or they may be the limitations of the given programming—rules that cannot be easily broken without altering the game's code. Though games may not yet have complete or *real* interactivity,[17] they do have their own ludic identity as a medium. The human subject must continuously choose new directions within the game in order for CMD to progress or to function at all. The necessity of the player/user/active subject is again the distinguishing characteristic of electronic/new media, especially interactive digital gaming.

3.3 Interview Data: Discourses of Fantasy vs. Reality

The following data emerged from the case study described in Chapter 1 that explored constructions of masculine identity through play practices of males who grew up in the 1980s (Cole, 2013, 2014). Due to popular conceptions that violent action/aggression is a result of game play with violent themes, many of the connections between virtual experience and reality are framed within this context. Interview participants were aware of this supposed connection[18] and framed their answers in response to it.

The use of language to describe traditionally male play activities as children aligned with boys' understanding or acceptance of similar activities in their work in their professional careers as adults (Cole, 2013). Male participants of similar age and professional background completed in-depth interviews that included examples *of* computer-mediated discourse as well as participants' discourse *about* CMD. Participants described their thoughts and feelings about various interactive digital media play activities. The discourses provide insight into the influences of fantasy through play on later perceptions of reality. Previous research focused on the physiological and psychological impacts of desensitization to violence through entertainment such as video games, film, and television.[19]

Adachi and Willoughby (2012) provided context for aggression beyond video game play, connecting other competitive acts such as gambling through a longitudinal study that focused on the competitive nature of video game play, rather than on violent game content, as the primary factor in short-term increases in aggression. Other competitive activities may be equally to blame for outcomes of aggression such as hostility or violence.[20] Additionally, it is important to consider that aggression is not always a problem, depending on the situation. Consider sports, for example, in which aggression is fostered and lauded; this may provide a new perspective on the effects of competitive interactive media play. The interview data provided in this book give voice to the participants in play, allowing them to contextualize their own experiences. I analyzed their responses through a pragmatics of verbal discourse regarding the influence of childhood interactive media game play.

Talk about game play regarding seemingly distinct categories, such as reality-versus-virtual reality and work-versus-play, was common to much of the discourse. The initial interviews addressed how adult men talk about experiences of real-life violence, how they talk about experiences of fictional violence, especially in terms of interactive media such as video games, and in what ways they connect, if at all, play practices of their youth with their understandings of reality as an adult. A clearer idea of how play or fantasy influences real perceptions, with discernible outcomes such as preferred career choice, was reached through an analysis of the ways men discuss their personal understandings of these cultural influences (Cole, 2013).

Expressions of broad cultural understandings with game-related overtones, such as social expectations to be able to play with (alter) their personality or physical appearance or engaging in incentive processes that reflect rule-based processes reminiscent of play in the work place, are examples of ludic identification (de Mul, 2005). Interview participants expressed a level of ludic identity in ways that implied its naturalization. Interview participants also alluded to ergodic identification, players' connections to characters on the screen (Carr, 2006). Yee (2014) examined the influence of virtual worlds and avatar identification on human players. This focus on the game realm serves an important role in understanding the influence of interactive media. Ergodic ontogeny builds on Yee's concepts to address the manner in which virtual experiences effect personal identity development. The following analysis incorporates gamers' talk about personal identity construction and virtual play experiences overall: the development of ergodic identity through the process of ergodic ontogeny.[21] Players described many aspects and influences of video game play, all of which reflect their own perceptions of self-identification within and beyond the interactive digital play experience.

The process of writing an in-depth, semi-structured interview is very natural—more like the script to a casual conversation on a topic, but with a detailed and intentional focus on the chosen research questions. Descriptions of the interview process with one participant (Levi) are provided here in pursuit of methodological transparency to serve as an example of the details of this process before delving into coding of linguistic data. The level of detail provided by an interview participant yields far more information than a survey or even focus group, because a single person is independently reflecting on personal experiences, thoughts, feelings, memories, and insights. This face-to-face interaction is more likely to evoke a detailed and thoughtful response from research participants and allows for further explanation after key points are made, so that it is more likely the researcher understands the intentions of responses accurately (Roulston, 2010).

My first interview was with a young man who had recently served four years in the United States military. He chose the pseudonym, Levi, a biblical name (the pious son of Jacob) referenced in many religious scriptures. Before the interview, when signing the consent form, Levi seemed to become slightly more wary—perhaps not having fully realized beforehand that there would be an *official* component to the interaction in terms of a contract. I explained that the form simply assured him the information from this interview session would only be used for specific research purposes and that his name and any identifying details would not be revealed. Despite having pre-set questions, the nature of a semi-structured interview process allows for interjection and rephrasing of questions into a more conversational tone.[22] In the case of Levi, the conversational nature of the interview was not immediate. The first few questions were markedly awkward, whether due to lack of familiarity or simply acclimation to the interview process.

The discussion and signing of the consent form was not recorded, but the rest of the interaction was digitally recorded for later transcription. Additionally, after the interview and recording ended, Levi spoke for a few minutes about how he felt discussing some of the more emotional aspects of the interview questions, especially related to his time in the military and his feelings about the violence he witnessed there. It was difficult not to become emotionally involved during this discussion. No interviewer is ever neutral or objective, and each brings personal experience and feelings of either empathy or discordance to such interactions. This is an unavoidable aspect of research that must be considered when valuing the data presented here, though it does not nullify or make this data any less meaningful/useful.[23]

Levi made connections between his interest in violent entertainment media and his level of comfort with real-life violence, though he always specified that the two were unrelated. Despite such assertions, many of his statements did imply a relationship.[24] Levi provided a number of enlightening insights into why he thinks people, especially young, "restless" as he called himself, American men are interested in violence,[25] how they respond to violent situations that are presented in different ways, and the connections between desensitization to violence in entertainment media and in reality.

Themes of denial were present in all interviewee responses. Like Levi, other participants did not want to link their interactive media experiences of violent game content to real-world conceptions.[26] Participants used linguistic devices to distance these concepts from one another and to assure the interviewer of players' ability to differentiate between fantasy and reality. Hyper-realistic portrayals of violence in modern media conjured memories of similar experiences in military and other settings for the participants in some cases. All interviewees expressed a clear delineation between their understanding and feelings about those types of fictional violence, even if reminiscent of genuine memories and actual lived experiences.

Discourse analysis of Levi's interview provided insight into the content of his responses, but the responses themselves are also meaningful windows into how he viewed play. During his interview, Levi explained that he did play video games as a child (as many young people of his generation did, especially males), and that the more violent the nature of the game, the more appealing it seemed. He discussed his participation in group game play as well as individual time spent gaming and the differences in his experience of violent themes in those regards. Generally, the more bloody or violent a game, the more popular it became for him and his male friends.[27]

Levi's preferred game was *GoldenEye: 007* (1997), a first-person shooter with relatively minimal blood and gore. Still, the purpose of the game is to kill your opponent, which requires shooting the virtual representation of another human being. *GoldenEye: 007* can be played as a single-player *story* mode, which Levi enjoyed, or a multiplayer *versus* mode[28] that took up many hours of his youth spent playing with friends.

The social aspect of video game play was an important factor in his interest in this activity, but he also spent time alone playing games. As he grew up, Levi's interest in video games continued, though time spent playing was limited due to other obligations (both professional and social). As an adult, he reported that he still gravitated toward games with violent themes and explained that he related this to conceptions of masculinity in the United States that feel, for him, ingrained.

In response to a question about the potential for underlying violent tendencies in his other hobbies, Levi pointed out that hunting was an interest that he relates to his enjoyment of weapons, but that he did not feel hunting was a violent act—rather an appreciation of nature—a distinction that many people might either disagree with or perhaps not have considered.[29] Addressing the idea that violence in films, video games,

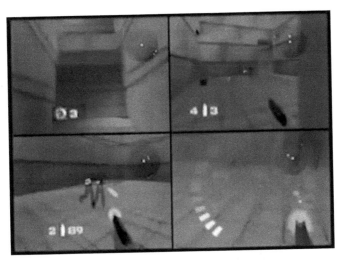

Figure 3.6 Screenshot of *GoldenEye: 007*. GoldenEye: 007 [Video game]. (1997). Kyoto, Japan: Nintendo.

books, or other media influence real-life acts of violence (school shootings or criminal activity, for example), Levi asserted that though there is some connection in the learning process (the military uses digital simulation in training exercises),[30] he believes the direct correlation of the two is grossly exaggerated.[31]

The interview switched topics midway in order to discuss participants' educational and professional background. At that point, Levi explained that directly after his completion of high school, he enlisted in the United States military. At the time of his enlistment, the U.S. was not actively engaged in any combat scenarios, but the possibility of going to war and the assured opportunity to learn skills used for killing others were primary contributing factors to his decision to join the armed forces. He explained this mindset in terms of slight naivety and also a connection to a patriotic duty to serve one's country. Levi's family had a history of military involvement in previous generations, and he did not want to see that disappear. This description, while accurate and honest, is complicated as it positions his interest in something that could be viewed as negative (violence and killing other human beings) in a culturally acceptable and commendable light (military service and family tradition).

Levi expressed a direct relationship between the video game *Call of Duty: Modern Warfare* (2007) and his experiences in the military. He commended the game repeatedly for the accuracy of its depictions of combat situations, the levels of blood, or other realistic injuries related to such scenarios. He described the sense of playing this game as "taking him right back" to his combat experiences. In fact, he stated that the only time he had dreams about his time overseas after returning home was while playing this game. Levi reported enjoying the game play because of this realistic quality, but also seemed to be troubled by the strong association with his real-life experience.

If post-traumatic stress indicators, like dreams of combat in wartime scenarios, present themselves only during interactive entertainment experiences with such high levels of immersion and realism, then the influence of these play experiences certainly warrants research from a number of disciplinary angles despite assertions from players that there is no meaningful connection between the game and reality. Games like *Battlefield I* (2016) take realism in game play to new levels, a trend that will likely only continue into the newest console generations, potentially evoking even stronger reactions from players than those discussed by Levi.

Levi spoke of situations while overseas in which he experienced violence first-hand and had to deal with the immediacy of the reality of a war zone. He described his emotional response to such incidents as an overwhelming sense of panic and fear and that in thinking back on them now, his reaction is one of sadness and a sinking feeling due to the loss of fellow soldiers and the taking of human life in general, which is not something he takes lightly. When asked if these experiences would help him attain a career in law enforcement (on the state or federal level) that he was pursuing, he stated yes.[32] He felt that he would be better equipped to deal with certain scenarios than other law enforcement officials who had not had the same experiences.

Figure 3.7 Realism in battle with QR Code. Battlefield IV [Video game]. (2013). Redwood City, CA: Electronic Arts. https://vimeo.com/185105533.

Levi admitted that although people *do* not, and *should* not, ever get used to the experience of violence in reality, it does get easier to cope with as you have more practice going through the necessary physical and emotional responses. He explained that this could be viewed as desensitization to violence in the same ways that playing a particularly gruesome part of a video game might desensitize a player to the images on the screen, but that the differences between one's reaction to fantasy and to reality are distinct. He argued that there is a clear and definable difference *for him*, and his response implied that he believed this to be true for all people, between enacting violence in a fantasy (video game) setting and in a real-life setting.

Though both popular and academic attacks on media attribute the enactment of real-world violence to *training* that takes place while participating in entertainment practices with violent thematic content, supposedly stemming from a desensitization through repeated exposure, there are a myriad of other possible variables for causes of these actions such as mental health issues, bullying, etc.[33] Interview participants reported engaging in interactive media with violent themes but do not connect these experiences directly to their tolerance for violence in reality as adults. Analyses of discourses of gaming do not necessarily require a discussion of game violence or its implications for real-world action. However, this topic seems to emerge more often than any other in news media coverage of video games (with the common focus on *shooters* or *military style* games). Therefore, any discussion of interactive media effects (whether individual ergodic ontogeny or more broad social trends) that ignores this subject will likely be cited as avoiding a controversial aspect of this medium. Addressing the stereotypes associated with video games, masculinity, and violence head-on is appropriate. Through a nuanced exploration of players' talk about game experiences, a more complex (less one-sided) argument can be formed for supporting some cultural stereotypes (of players and games) while disproving others. Direct topical analysis of interactive media discourses provides a basic foundation for understanding the ergodic ontogenetic process as expressed in ways that are both familiar and in need of continued scrutiny.

3.4 Personalized Concepts and Experiences of Play

Interview participants reported that play activity, including the watching or playing (enacting, performing) of violent media, has an emotional connection to experiences of real-life violence, but not a causal effect. One participant's response, provided below, was unsolicited. The interview focused on interactive digital gaming practices, and a question regarding professional real-life experiences prompted the following excerpt—broken down here according to pragmatics (coding and analysis as explained in Chapter 1). Analyzing the details of this response provided insight into the meaning of this discourse beyond the simple reporting of the content of his speech as in the previous example of Levi's interview.

When describing experiences of real-life violence, many participants' discourse reflected a marked shift in tone from the rest of the interview process. For example, when describing a memory of violence in his profession, another participant, George, referenced the difference between games and reality.

George's response:

1. G: I ran the gambit of video games that were extremely violent
2. G: that had the blood splatter (2)
3. G: but at the same time, I do remember having played those games
4. G: and seeing all that, and even though I still had the stomach for it
5. G: I remember being like 'gee' (.)
6. G: there's a severed head (3) in real life
7. G: or 'gee', uh (.) this one particular time
8. G: I went to go check on welfare for someone
9. G: hadn't heard from this person for days (.)
10. G: and there might have been some (1)
11. G: psychological problems and things like that.
12. G: But all the tell-tale signs that there was a (1)
13. G: of the person being dead inside the house were there (2)
14. G: And finally I remember opening that door (.)
15. G: and the stench (.)
16. G: and finally getting to the room where it was,
17. G: cuz what had happened was a guy took a rifle to (.) um (1)
18. G: under his chin (.) and you know (.)
19. G: blew his own head off (2)
20. G: And it, it, obliterated his head.
21. G: I mean, there was an eyeball in his lap,
22. G: and just seeing that in real life.
23. G: And smelling it in real life (1)
24. G: it was still very shocking for me (.)
25. G: And do I feel like games desensitized it for me?
26. G: No...No.

A marked shift in tone between play or fantasy with terms like "blood splatter" (line 2) and "real life" (lines 6, 22, and 23) is obvious in this discourse. Line 2 has a two second pause after the word "splatter," a distinct rest during which the speaker was perhaps self-reflective or thinking about instances outside of a game environment in which that term was relevant. Similarly, the repetition of "real life" implies the importance of this distinction to the speaker and the desire for clarity of expression to the interviewer on this topic above others.

The serious tone of description in the sentences related to his finding of the dead man stresses the reality of emotion in this situation in comparison to his earlier discussion of fictional violence. Inclusion of details like "stench" (line 15) and "smell" (line 23) distinguish this experience from virtual (fictional) violence that as yet does not incorporate this sense. Sentence length, short distinct phrases, and the placement of the speaker's hesitating "um" (line 17) before describing the position of the rifle communicate his discomfort and agitation in reliving and sharing this memory. The repetition and stress of the words "in real life" (three times) and "no" (twice in succession in line 26) at the end of the statement are particularly poignant. Participants demonstrated complex processes of self-identification in terms of moral ideologies regarding violence and death, as evidenced by nuanced switches between discussions of violence in play and in reality, that reflect the need to deny any playful aspect to the realities they experience in their work.

Distinguishing between fantasy and reality often comes down to conceptions of work versus play. Even if an experience happens in the real world (non-virtual), it can be dismissed to a certain extent if it happens in the context of an experience that is *just a game* or if the experience is part of *play*. Csikszentmihalyi (1975)[34] described enjoyment of activities that are not unpleasant or tedious and have intrinsic motivation. Working for outcomes outside of intrinsic motivation supports the work/play dichotomy and furthers a sense that the end goal is the only justification for our actions.[35] He explained that his goal was to "understand enjoyment, here and now—not as compensation for past desires, not as preparation for future needs, but as an ongoing process that provides rewarding experiences in the present" (Csikszentmihalyi, 1975, p. 9)—a play experience well suited to analyses of computer-mediated interactive games that rely on immediate experience. He focused on autotelic activities, those that "required formal and extensive energy output on the part of the actor, yet provided few if any conventional rewards" (Csikszentmihalyi, 1975, p. 10), again processes easily paralleling the non-trivial effort of video game play experience that lack many tangible or immediate real-world benefits in the traditional sense.

This is distinct from concepts of *game flow* that refer to the progression of the game and the game design that users experience. In this use of the term, players gain satisfaction and gratification from performing well within the game realm, but there are no real-world benefits (other than potentially communal prestige or improved mental acuity) to pursuing these levels of play. Enjoyment, like play, is located outside of reality, a state of experience that is "not accessible in 'everyday life'" (Csikszentmihalyi, 1975, p. 35), with specific psychological frames of expectations that outline the differences between the two. *Flow* is a state "poised between boredom and worry" (Csikszentmihalyi, 1975, p. 35–36). This expression of play is rule bound, with an internal reward system in feeling a sense of comfort while also obtaining satisfaction through successful action.

The necessary merging of action and awareness is most practicable in activities with "clearly established rules of action" making the activity feasible, within one's ability to perform; the player must be able to control the outcome to a certain extent while centering one's attention "on a limited stimulus field" often to the point of forgetting ego (Csikszentmihalyi, 1975, p. 39–40). Though applied to play states more generally, this description nearly perfectly mirrors interactivity in computer/console games. Playing an interactive, digital game can be an example of *flow* but does not guarantee this experience. There must be some incentive to join a game based on competition, gain, or danger, but the primary factor must be internal.[36] A video game might induce players through graphics or other enticements, but ultimately it is the play experience that must be satisfying if repeat or continuous play is to occur.

This is an important distinction in terms of the interviewee's comments. If they experience situations in a virtual environment, ideally in a state of flow, then they may form a strong connection to that experience that lends itself to interpretation beyond the game world. This form of interaction with media content is what may lead to moments of internalization of game content that influences players' sense of self and ideology during and beyond experiences of play—the process of ergodic ontogeny. They may also, whether experiencing a flow state or not, distinguish between play experiences and work experiences and choose to avoid conscious connections between the two, as evidenced by George's remarks in the last example. The ways in which players understand the context of their experiences are tied to elements of visual and new media literacy. The modes through which data is shared with players changes their internalization and learning processes during play. This process relies on complex systems of understanding multimodal texts that are often reported as being only subconscious, seeming innate, and a natural progression of modern literacy practices.

Language is no longer bound to terms of speech and text. We must examine how these older modes of communication operate within the current multimodal framework that incorporates image, sound, and interactivity. Modes of communication and understanding are "inseparable from cultural and from social but also…from affective and cognitive matters" (Kress, 2004, p. 59); all meaning is signified in terms of its maker who then relies on the other to interpret and create new meaning. Kress' concept of multimodal meaning-making drives "the emergent creation of qualitatively new forms of meaning as a result of 'shifting' ideas across semiotic modes" (Nelson, 2006, p. 58).[37] Communication is constantly changing and technology is linked to those changes. Nelson (2006) used the term *multi-competent* to describe the growing necessity of working multimodally in the highest levels of personal expression.

The ways in which players talk about interactive media play experiences and also about discourses of gaming are critical elements in the larger puzzle of interactive media influence and multimodal literacy/competency. Pursuit of better means of understanding these influences is increasingly important as societies are now more often defined in terms of their production of information and learning, rather than tangible material products.[38] Learning cultures are becoming more interactive, multimodal, and dispersed across a range of media and locations.

Reflexivity for users of digital media, as technology becomes more accessible,[39] provides a means of expression that fosters intuitive self-attention leading to moments of personal revelation.[40] Pedagogical shifts[41] increasingly place students in the role of media maker and consumer.[42] Educators continue to combine technologies,[43] positioning students as meaning makers in the modern context.[44] The depth of connection to information forged through agentive action, whether creating a media form or playing through one with a particular sense of independence or intent, supports the conception that ergodic ontogeny is an integral step in modern mental development that will only increase as interactive digital gaming is available to more of the world population and maintains its place as the most profitable (popular) and immersive (influential) communicative form.

Computer-mediated discourse shapes individuals' understandings of texts and the potentials for authorship and experiences of narrative. Despite the variety of forms of text, hypertext, interactive environments, and stimuli, players' interview data supported an internalized social sense of what is most appropriate to share about their experiences of video game play.[45] Different expressions of ergodic ontogeny inform the realities of play experience and the learning processes that result from digital media interactivity.

Notes

1 "Digital visual media ... honor, rival, and revise linear-perspective painting, photography, film, television, and print. No medium today...seems to do its cultural work in isolation from other media, any more than it works in isolation from other social and economic forces" (Bolter & Grusin, 2000, p. 15).

2 As Bolter and Grusin (2000) articulated it, "our culture wants both to multiply its media and to erase all traces of mediation: ideally, it wants to erase its media in the very act of multiplying them" (p. 5).

3 Also see Syvertsen and Ytreberg (2006).

4 Bolter and Grusin (2000) applied Foucault's genealogy of descent to new media literacy, stating that our genealogical traits are "immediacy, hypermediacy, and remediation; however, where Foucault was concerned with relations of power, our proposed genealogy is defined by the formal relations within and among media as well as by relations of cultural power and prestige" (p. 21). This is not exclusive to interactive entertainment media

gaming, though video games do provide a clear example of the immediacy of remediation.

5 A limitation of their analysis is the focus on pre-teen male players and the limited functions of game narrative in broader culture, a discrepancy likely due to the great strides in video game ubiquity and influence over the last decades since their writing.

6 Most games strive for cinematic representation over reality. Game developers at Crytek discussed immersion and escapism in a video interview for *The Atlantic,* here: http://www.theatlantic.com/video/index/265778/videogames-get-cinematic/.

7 Manovich's method is *digital materialism* in which theory is built from the ground up to "scrutinize the principles of computer hardware and software and the operations involved in creating cultural objects on a computer to uncover a new cultural logic at work" (p. 10). He is critical of the accuracy of words like *digital* and *interactivity* as they are too broad to be useful without qualification. Yet, these are the primary terminology at our disposal if the intent is to share ideas about this medium with a wide audience. Therefore, despite the complicated or bulky inclusion of qualifiers, these terms are the best option available for quickly conveying the concept of narrative-driven video-based ergodic game experiences. Manovich acknowledges that "a particularly important example of how computer games use – and extend – cinematic language is their implementation of a dynamic point of view" such as automatic replays from a number of angles or the ability to adjust the POV (p. 84).

8 A project exploring such concepts of transmedia storytelling is the "User Engagement and Interaction Analytics in Transmedia Narratives" at the University of Amsterdam.

9 Multiliteracies and metalanguage are theoretical areas that involve exploration of the relationship between image and text in terms of multimodal negotiations within new media (Burn, 2008; Holmes, 1995; Kress & Van Leeuwen, 2001; Unsworth, 2008).

10 Kress (2000) worked toward a new theory of semiosis that acknowledged recent changes and adaptations to the structures of language, a code he argued must be "founded on a recognition of the 'interested action' of socially located, culturally and historically formed individuals, as the remakers, the transformers, and the re-shapers of the representational resources available to them" (p. 155).

11 Kress (2000) argued that "the single, exclusive and intensive focus on written language has dampened the full development of all kinds of human potentials, through all the sensorial possibilities of human bodies, in all kinds of respects, cognitively and affectively, in two- and three-dimensional representation" (p. 157). Hypertext fictions certainly refute such claims, as do multi-authored texts and even reading machines. See http://www.readies.org/. Traditional text is transformed or operates outside of limiting structure in many cases.

12 Daisley (1994) discussed the game of literacy with a focus on the empowering capabilities of games as teaching tools when students are engaged in creating the rules of play. Still relevant in terms of computer-mediated communication (CMC), Daisley explained that "dismissing 'playfulness' and 'gaming' as being nonproductive may, by implication, lead students to think that there is nothing pleasurable about experimental discourse and practicing literacy skills" (p. 107).

13 Her conclusion was that IBMs were preferable for introducing students to academic discourse. Macs were less preferable despite having very similar capabilities.

14 The concept of *game* is a subcategory of *play*, but "as Gadamer notices in his phenomenological analysis of play in *Truth and Method*, play has its own, even sacred, seriousness" (1989, p. 102), reminiscent of an experience of *flow*—the idea that during play, the player floats between reality and fantasy but still applies a sense of urgency and realism to in-game experiences; the player has to care while still finding the experience pleasurable. Play only fulfills its purpose if the player "loses himself in play" (Raessens & Goldstein, 2005, p. 257).

15 de Mul builds upon Ricoeur's theory of narrative identity, which (in conflict with Descartes and Heidegger) posits that we do not "have an immediate access to the self in introspection or phenomenological intuition. Self-knowledge is in almost all cases mediated" (Raessens & Goldstein, 2005, p. 253). "Because [Ricoeur's] theory exclusively focuses on standard linguistic narratives," de Mul amended it to apply "within the domain of computer games" (Raessens & Goldstein, 2005, p. 251).

16 This follows Huizinga's definition that a game is "a free act that takes place within a specially designated time in a specially designated place, according to specific rules which are strictly adhered to' (Huizinga, 1970, p. 13)" (Raessens & Goldstein, 2005, p. 257).

17 Interactivity is understood here as "'the ability to intervene in a meaningful way within the representation itself, not to read it differently' (Cameron, 1995)" (Raessens & Goldstein, 2005, p. 259).

18 They addressed this concern despite the fact that the idea of real violence as a result of game violence was not explicitly mentioned during the interview briefing.

19 See Bartholow, Bushman, and Sestir (2006), Carnagey, Anderson, and Bushman (2007), Cline, Croft, and Courrier (1973), Funk, Baldacci, Pasold, and Baumgardner (2004), and Linz, Donnerstein, and Adams (1989), among others.

20 DeLisi, Vaughn, Gentile, Anderson, and Shook (2013) reported results, though preliminary, that demonstrated a correlation between violent video game exposure and violent criminal behavior. A direct correlation or causal relationship was not established, but they suggested that "violent video game exposure may be one risk factor for delinquency" (DeLisi et al., 2013, p. 138). Ivory and Kaestle (2013) explored the "effects of profanity used by protagonist and antagonist characters in a 'first person shooter' game" and found "profanity used by both protagonist and antagonist characters increased hostile expectations, a direct precursor to aggressive behaviors" (p. 224). An important distinction in this study is that they addressed profanity in game content, not aggressive language used by players. Lin (2013) compared the role of violent or aggressive content across media, finding that indeed "media interactivity in video games exacerbated the violent effect on short-term, aggressive responses" and that "character identification did not mediate the effect of media interaction on aggression" (p. 535).

21 Again, this is defined as the ways in which ludic and ergodic identification lead to immersive play experiences, which, in conjunction with narrative, ludic elements and programming, influence the identity and ideology of players beyond the game world.

22 There are also occasions when it is beneficial to vary slightly from the list of interview topics in order to avoid asking repeat question should a participant have already covered certain topics adequately.

23 The valuing of data based on personal experience is described in feminist theory. Stone-Mediatore (1998) described stories of experiences as problematic in that they "risk naturalizing ideologically conditioned categories

that structure our experiences of self and world," but many leading theorists would be undermined if this idea were accepted entirely (p. 116). She argued that narratives are limited by modern readings of texts merely as "reports of unreflective consciousness," which obscures the "more subtle ways they emerge from and affect historical experience" (Stone-Mediatore, 1998, p. 117). Truth is mediated through experience, as Haraway expressed in the form of the "discovery that visual experience is not mere reception of reality but an active process informed by expectations" (Stone-Mediatore, 1998, p. 117). Harding, Hennessy, and Smith also valued marginal experience narratives because "experience-oriented writing brings into public discussion questions and concerns excluded in dominant ideologies, ideologies which sustain and are sustained by political and economic hierarchies" (Stone-Mediatore, 1998, p. 126). Our language is "vulnerable to further disruption or appropriation" even as we are self-reflexive (Stone-Mediatore, 1998, p. 130).

24 For example, Levi provided the example of his military training (simulation) in which soldiers have to shoot at human-shaped targets that drop in realistic ways in order to get used to firing on other people.

25 Levi related these interests to a naïve belief in invincibility that he did not link directly to media consumption habits, but rather to internalized and natural cultural norms in Western society that cultivate and foster this sense in young males, especially around the age at which the armed services begin their recruiting (late teens).

26 This is similar to concepts of identity dissonance in interview data found by Brown (1999) who reported expressions of disconnection between feelings of self and expectations of society, but focused on young female discourse. Brown described how disavowal of expected social ills is part of structural narrative, ideologies and discourses juxtaposed. She explored the impulse to tell particular kinds of stories with certain kinds of features, requisite disavowal, and the idea that certain gestures in story are ideologically important.

27 The direct correlation between aggression and video game play is scrutinized because players bring certain elements of identity with them to the media they consume. Cultural and personal factors certainly play a role in media influence. Anderson et al. (2010) cited a "panel of experts assembled by the U.S. Surgeon General" who stated that "research on violent television and films, video games, and music reveals unequivocal evidence that media violence increases the likelihood of aggressive and violent behavior in both immediate and long-term context," findings that are supported by many other reputable institutions including the APA and U.S. Department of Health and Human Services (p. 152). Cultural factors, such as the way violence is portrayed with or without attention to the suffering of the victim, have more effect on viewers than the amount of violence displayed. Due to the limited number of studies of video game violence, compared to those researching film and television, there are also meta-analyses that suggest that "the effects of violent video games on aggression have been substantially overestimated because of publication bias," but these meta-analyses may themselves be methodologically flawed (Anderson et al., 2010, p. 152).

28 In this form of game play, players share the screen while each maneuvers a character via individual controller to navigate a shared play space/setting in attempts to destroy one another and be the *last man standing*.

29 There are multiple cultural differences in aggression, and in the inhibition and reporting of violence or crime.

30 Examples can be found at http://www.goarmy.com/downloads/games.html.

31 There are short- and long-term effects of video game play. Short-term effects include "priming existing knowledge structures" that might instigate aggression when a game contains similar scripts (even if they lack any "surface-level similarity" between game and reality) (Anderson et al., 2010, p. 155). Mimicry and "observational learning of new behaviors and beliefs about their likely success" are other short-term effects. Long-term effects, results that can be understood in terms of ergodic ontogeny, result "from relatively permanent changes in beliefs, expectancies, scripts, attitudes and other related personal factors that are brought about by repeated exposure to video game violence" through "repeated exposure to violent media [that] is expected to lead to measurable changes in the chronic accessibility of aggression-related knowledge structures" (Anderson et al., 2010, p. 155). Yet, cultural influences cannot be ignored: "some cultures are relatively supportive of certain types of violence, whereas other cultures condemn them" (Anderson et al., 2010, p. 155). The multiple determining factors involved with true long-term increases in aggressive behavior make it difficult to pinpoint video game play as the cause of increases in violence in society. Games without violent content are predicted to have no effect on increased aggression. Puri and Pugliese (2012) used survey data to examine video game playing aggression in terms of sex, type of game played, and length of play among college students and found no statistically significant relationships between aggression and sex or length of play; however, "significant differences were found in levels of aggression between playing and nonplaying respondents of action role-playing...and role-playing video games" with those playing RPGs exhibiting decreased levels of aggression, perhaps due to the empathy involved in taking on the pursuits/goals of the character on the screen in a more personal way, a clear counter to suggestions that violent play always increases aggression to some extent (p. 345).

32 Levi stated that the skills and combat experience of the Marine Corps make him better suited to this line of work and prepared him for difficult, violent situations that might arise in his field.

33 See Birkland and Lawrence (2009), Burns and Crawford (1999), Elliot (2009), Feshbach and Singer (1971), and Leary, Kowalski, Smith, and Phillips (2003).

34 *Beyond Boredom and Anxiety* (Csikszentmihalyi, 1975) details some differences between work and play and provides insight into ways of recognizing play as it happens.

35 Csikszentmihalyi's (1975) study looked at "activities that appear to contain rewards within themselves, that do not rely on scarce material incentives... activities that are ecologically sound" (p. 5) yet are considered *unproductive*. Most scholarship focused on the "social or psychological function of intrinsically rewarding activities rather than in the enjoyable experience itself" (p. 7), and Csikszentmihalyi criticized the limitations of psychology in dealing with creativity, religion, and enjoyment of complex activities.

36 Csikszentmihalyi (1975) admitted that "most people need some inducement to participate in flow activities, at least at the beginning, before they learn to be sensitive to intrinsic rewards" (p. 42).

37 Nelson (2006) discussed Barthes' idea of a "multidimensional [text] in which a variety of writings, none of them original, blend and clash," accepting that there may be no new stories but that "we can authentically redesign or...populate the utterances of others with our 'own intentions'" (p. 57).

38 We rely on Information Communication Technologies (ICTs) as leverage for economic development and societal survival and must not underestimate

"that the discourse of knowledge society [has]...a 'reality effect' in that sense that it has decisive commercial and policy implications in many parts of the world" (Drotner, 2008, p. 66).

39 Mods of games like *Never Winter Nights* (Cole, 2011) are available for PC users, but examples such as Pixel Press are even more open to creativity; see http://projectpixelpress.com/.

40 Many games, even if not mods, incorporate an element of introspective storytelling, veering away from traditional game play elements. Some examples include *Catherine* (2011), *Dear Esther* (2008, 2012), *The Stanley Parable* (2011), and *Nier* (2010).

41 See Lambert (2009), Nelson, Hull, and Roche-Smith (2008), and Sandars, Murray, and Pellow (2008).

42 A forthcoming project (Cole/Pittore 2017) explores the therapeutic and educational potential of Digital Storytelling workshops that create simple interactive playable game narratives as opposed to the short videos produced in traditional DS Workshops (Lambert, 2009).

43 As these changes take place, students will ideally work *with* academic content rather than *for* it, coming to their own understandings and discoveries resulting in deeper, more lasting connections with the material.

44 The educational aspects of serious games should not be ascribed only to young learners. For example, the Serious Games Initiative is "focused on uses for games in exploring management and leadership challenges facing the public sector" (http://www.seriousgames.net/).

45 Participants expressed this social awareness through distancing and denial of causal links between play and reality (avoiding the popular misrepresentations of gamers) as well as through potential modifiers in speech and content due to an interview process led by a female researcher. More information about the complex concerns of social science research can be found in Chapter 6.

References

Aarseth, E. (1999). Aporia and epiphany in Doom and The Speaking Clock: The temporality of ergodic art. In M.-L Ryan (Ed.), *Cyberspace textuality: Computer technology and literary theory*. Bloomington, IN: Indiana University Press.

Adachi, P. J., & Willoughby, T. (2012). Do video games promote positive youth development? *Journal of Adolescent Research, 28*(2), 155–165.

Anderson, C. A., Shibuya, A., Ihori, N., Swing, E. L., Bushman, B. J., Sakamoto, A., ... Saleem, M. (2010). Violent video game effects on aggression, empathy, and prosocial behavior in eastern and western countries: A meta-analytic review. *Psychological Bulletin, 136*(2), 151–173.

Bartholow, B. D., Bushman, B. J., & Sestir, M. A. (2006). Chronic violent video game exposure and desensitization to violence: Behavioral and event-related brain potential data. *Journal of Experimental Social Psychology, 42*(4), 532–539. doi:10.1016/j.jesp.2005.08.006.

Baym, N. (1996). Agreements and disagreements in a computer-mediated discussion. *Research on Language and Social Interaction, 29*(4), 315–345.

Birkland, T. A., & Lawrence, R. G. (2009). Media framing and policy change after Columbine. *American Behavioral Scientist, 52*(10), 1405–1425.

Bolter, J. D., & Grusin, R. (2000). *Remediation: Understanding new media.* Cambridge, MA: MIT Press.

Brown, L. M. (1999). *Raising their voices: The politics of girls' anger.* Cambridge, MA: Harvard University Press.

Burn, A. (2008). The case of rebellion: Researching multimodal texts. In J. Coiro, M.Knobel, C. Lankshear, & D. J. Leu (Eds.), *The handbook of research on new literacies* (p. 151–178). New York, NY: Erlbaum/Taylor & Francis.

Burns, R. & Crawford, C. (1999). School shootings, the media, and public fear: Ingredients for a moral panic. *Crime, Law and Social Change, 32*(2), 147–168.

Carnagey, N. L., Anderson, C. A., & Bushman, B. J. (2007). The effect of video game violence on physiological desensitization to real-life violence. *Journal of Experimental Social Psychology, 43*(3), 489–496. doi:10.1016/j.jesp.2006.05.003.

Carr, D. (2006). *Computer games: Text, narrative and play.* Cambridge, UK: Polity.

Cline, V. B., Croft, R. G., & Courrier, S. (1973). Desensitization of children to television violence. *Journal of Personality and Social Psychology, 27*(3), 360–365. doi:10.1037/h0034945.

Cole, S. (2011). (re)Designing meaningful play: Never winter Nights mod pilot study proposal, Virtual Worlds Graduate UnSymposium: Games, Play & Community, 2011. www.vw.unsymposium.org.

Cole, S. (2013). Discourses of masculinity: Culture, identity and violence. In D. Boswell, R. O'Shea and E. Tzadik (Eds.), *Interculturalism, meaning and identity* (p. 153–164). Oxford, UK: Inter-Disciplinary Press.

Cole, S. (2014). Gender identity construction through talk about video games. Special issue: New works on electronic literature and cyberculture. *CLC Web: Comparative Literature and Culture, 15*(16.5). Retrieved from http://dx.doi.org/10.7771/1481-4374.2487.

Csikszentmihalyi, M. (1975). *Beyond boredom and anxiety.* San Francisco, CA: Jossey-Bass Publishers.

Daisley, M. (1994). The game of literacy: The meaning of "play" in computer-mediated communication. *Computers and Composition, 11*(2), 107–119.

Danielewski, M. Z. (2000). *House of leaves: By Zampanò.* New York, NY: Pantheon Books.

DeLisi, M., Vaughn, M. G., Gentile, D. A., Anderson, C. A., & Shook, J. J. (2013). Violent video games, delinquency, and youth violence: New evidence. *Youth Violence and Juvenile Justice, 11*(2), 132–142.

De Mul, J. (2005). *The game of life: Narrative and ludic identity formation in computer games.* Retrieved from http://www.digra.org/dl/.

Drotner, K. (2008). Boundaries and bridges: Digital storytelling in education studies and media studies. In K. Lundby (Ed.), *Digital storytelling, mediatized stories* (p. 61–81). New York, NY: Peter Lang.

Feshbach, S., & Singer, R. D. (1971). *Television and aggression.* San Francisco, CA: Jossey-Bass Inc.

Elliott, D. (2009). Lessons from Columbine: Effective school-based violence prevention strategies and programmes. *Journal of Children's Services, 4*(4), 53–62.

Funk, J. B., Baldacci, H. B., Pasold, T., & Baumgardner, J. (2004). Violence exposure in real-life, video games, television, movies, and the internet: Is there desensitization? *Journal of Adolescence, 27*(1), 23–39. doi:10.1016/j. adolescence.2003.10.005.

Herring, S. (2001). Computer-mediated discourse. In D. Schiffrin, D. Tannen, & H. Hamilton (Eds.), *The handbook of discourse analysis* (p. 612–634). Malden, MA: Blackwell Publishers.

Holmes, M. E. (1995). Naming virtual space in computer-mediated conversation: New media analysis. *ETC: A Review of General Semantics, 52*(2), 212–221.

Ivory, A., & Kaestle, C. (2013). The effects of profanity in violent video games on players' hostile expectations, aggressive thoughts and feelings, and other responses. *Journal of Broadcasting & Electronic Media, 57*(2), 224–241.

Juul, J. (2011). *Half-real: Video games between real rules and fictional worlds.* Cambridge, MA: MIT Press.

Kress, G. (2000). Design and transformation: New theories of meaning. In B. Kope & M. Kalantzis (Eds.), *Multiliteracies: Literacy learning and the design of social futures* (p. 153–161). London, UK: Routledge.

Kress, G. (2004). *Literacy in the new media age.* New York, NY: Routledge.

Kress, G., & Van Leeuwen, T. (2001). *Multimodal discourse.* New York, NY: Bloomsbury Academic.

Lambert, J. (2009). *Digital storytelling: Capturing lives, creating community.* Berkeley, CA: Digital Diner Press.

Leary, M. R., Kowalski, R. M., Smith, L., & Phillips, S. (2003). Teasing, rejection, and violence: Case studies of the school shootings. *Aggressive Behavior, 29*(3), 202–214.

Lin, J.-H. (2013). Do video games exert stronger effects on aggression than film? The role of media interactivity and identification on the association of violent content and aggressive outcomes. *Computers in Human Behavior, 29*(3), 535–543.

Linz, D., Donnerstein, E., & Adams, S. M. (1989). Physiological desensitization and judgments about female victims of violence. *Human Communication Research, 15*(4), 509–522. doi:10.1111/j.1468-2958.1989.tb00197.x.

Manovich, L. (2002). *The language of new media.* Cambridge, MA: MIT Press.

Nelson, M. E. (2006). Mode, meaning, and synaesthesia in multimedia L2 writing. *Language Learning & Technology, 10*(2), 56–76.

Nelson, M. E., Hull, G. A., & Roche-Smith, J. (2008). Challenges of multimedia self-presentation. *Written Communication, 25*(4), 415–440.

Poster, M. (2001). *The information subject: Critical voices in art, theory and culture.* Amsterdam, Netherlands: G&B Arts International.

Puri, K., & Pugliese, R. (2012). Sex, lies, and video games: Moral panics or uses and gratifications. *Bulletin of Science, Technology & Society, 32*(5), 345–352.

Raessens, J., & Goldstein, J. (Eds.). (2005). *Handbook of computer game studies.* Cambridge, MA: MIT Press.

Roulston, K. J. (2010). *Reflective interviewing: A guide to theory and practice.* Thousand Oaks, CA: Sage Publications.

Ryan, M.-L. (1999). *Cyberspace textuality: Computer technology and literary theory.* Bloomington, IN: Indiana University Press.

Ryan, M.-L. (Ed.). (2004). *Narrative across media: The languages of storytelling*. Lincoln, NE: University of Nebraska Press.

Sandars, J., Murray, C., & Pellow, A. (2008). Twelve tips for using digital storytelling to promote reflective learning by medical students. *Medical Teacher*, *30*(8), 774–777.

Stone-Mediatore, S. (1998). Chandra Mohanty and the revaluing of "experience." *Hypatia*, *13*(2), 116–133.

Syvertsen, T., & Ytreberg, E. (2006). Participation and play in converging media. *NORDICOM Review*, *27*(1), 107–110.

Unsworth, L. (2008). Multiliteracies and metalanguage: Describing image/text relations as a resource for negotiating multimodal texts. In J. Coiro, M. Knobel, C. Lankshear, & D. J. Leu (Eds.), *The handbook of research on new literacies* (p. 377–405). London, UK: Routledge.

Yee, N. (2014). *The Proteus paradox: How online games and virtual worlds change us – and how they don't*. New Haven, CT: Yale University Press.

4 New Literacies

...even if we adopt the widest (and weakest) possible notion of narratives...an ontological difference would still remain...choice. In a game there must be choice.

—Espen Aarseth (Ryan, 2004, p. 366)

4.1 Interactive Digital Games as Cultural Narrative and Imagination

Computer and video games are both hailed and admonished for their influence on the ideological constructs of players, but our understandings of the ways narrative functions through these game experiences are still evolving. The term *narrative* is not universal or concrete in its definitions though "the ability to narrate is generally considered to be available to all human beings regardless of gender, race, colour, or cultural milieu (Barthes, 1977), and Bruner has suggested that we have a 'predisposition'" for narrative (Bruner, 2003, p. 33). People use stories to share ideas with others, tell personal experiences, entertain one another, pass on traditions, and define their lived experiences in narrative terms, often relying on plot and structure found outside the actual experiences being shared but framed within a classical narrative format for ease of communication and common understanding.

The idea that humans are predisposed toward narrative suggests that there is "something built in, something hardwired, that allows for this ubiquity" (Hazel, 2008, p. 200). We understand our experiences in narrative forms, according to calendars and timetables (the 24-hour day, appropriate times for meals, work, play, etc.) according to established patterns that are mirrored in narratives of a given culture and are all equally constructed by our own conscious choices. The narratives that are most prevalent and ingrained in a society influence how its people understand (experience and remember) lived moments. It is important to situate this discussion within wider knowledge of the complexities of cultural narratives in modern societies, like the United States, in terms of what it means if something is prevalent and ingrained. Cultural master narratives, or the dominant and hegemonic narratives, operate in relation to counter and oppositional narratives. Inclusion of counter-narratives in games may bring this relationship to light. Reliance on dominant narratives may also highlight the lack of equitable representation of groups based on race, culture, gender, sexual preference, or other factors that directly contest the narratives of a game.

Hazel (2008) stated that there are specific brain functions and systems of memory creation and relation that support an intrinsic human need[1] for narrative structure. Narratives in electronic or digital entertainment provide similar cultural functions as oral narratives in past cultures and serve as models for *normal* or *conventional* behavior. The more common the play of video games becomes, the more the narratives chosen for inclusion in video games will both influence and reflect the cultural traditions and mores of the time, resulting in influence on individuals' identity, ideology, and sociocultural knowledge (the process of ergodic ontogeny). "In this sense, these narratives absorbed and internalized from the culture are an indelible part of our identity" (Hazel, 2008, p. 204).[2] Storytelling as a form of meaning-making takes place in various communicative acts. Narrative analysis can be applied across disciplines to explore the connecting layers of meaning in broader social relations because many disciplines address issues of content, story, and plot. Narrativizing experiences serves various functions, such as framing new experiences in terms of older memories to make sense of the unknown, comforting and quelling extreme emotional responses by relating experiences to fables and tales with more positive outlooks, or distancing oneself from reality to ease tensions, fears, or anxieties.

Talk about experiences of trauma or other emotional distress, for example, is very specific in its form and function and is related to the way narrative shares and shapes emotional responses in other media forms. Sandberg and Tollefsen's (2010) analysis of talk about fear and violence in a community explored the ways in which "stories may create order in disturbing experiences and give meaning to major events or crises" and explained that "to tell about an experience can be a way to 'embody the self in stories' in settings where the self is being disembodied (e.g. in medical examinations, or in cases of rape or other types of physical violence)" (p. 2).[3] Using Labov's model (Labov & Waletzky, 1967), they found that fear and vulnerability are deeply tied to gender, resulting in a change in the public discourse in media and between individuals.[4]

Labov's model breaks down stories told about experiences with a focus on the order of the *told* versus the order of the *telling*. This method lacks criteria for analysis of evaluation (self-commentary on the events told) and is therefore decontextualized (does not take into account how people structure their own personal narratives). Labov's technique addressed how people structure their personal narratives but limited what is considered a meaningful part of that narrative. Women generally express greater fear of violence than do men, despite the *fear-risk paradox*,[5] and are more willing and able to tell about these experiences than men are. Male discourses of fear are distanced and fragmented with less impulse or ability to tell. Analysis of the structure of stories, impulses to tell, and what kinds of situated people *have* an impulse to tell have meaningful implications for interviews of male interactive digital media participants.

Games can provide narrative and ludic approaches to self-improvement and mental clarity, as explained in *SuperBetter* (McGonigal, 2015). *SuperBetter* (2012) is also the name of the game designed to aid in recovery from mental and physical stresses or injuries.

The ways in which discourse and narrative frames operate in interpersonal and media communication change the way the person receiving information interprets this data. Narrative can also change expectations of what a communicative act indicates about the narrator. If the creation of narratives (for a variety of purposes) is a hard-wired, natural aspect of discourse, then how do interactive digital game narratives influence the telling of real and/or virtual experiences? Narrative elements that are unique to video games are another essential lens through which interactive media influence must be viewed.

Narrative in media, especially in entertainment forms like video games, is linked closely to the concept of *narrative imagination* discussed by Von Wright (2002).[6] Von Wright argued that in order for one to become a *cultivated world citizen*, "critical thinking and narrative imagination must not only deal with verbal and intellectual argumentation but must also confront emotions and habits so that we are genuinely affected, touched" (p. 408). This speaks to the way in which players might invest themselves in game narratives and therefore change their own personal

Figure 4.1 Screenshot of *SuperBetter*. SuperBetter [Video game]. (2012). Retrieved from https://www.superbetter.com/.

viewpoints[7] beyond the game as well. Literature plays a central role in developing narrative imagination, but the (w)/reading taking place for many people in modern society may very well be the application of new media literacy/electracy[8] onto cultural artifacts or *texts* (other than text-based written/typed documents), including interactive digital games.

Literature provides foundation terminology for the study of interactive digital play *texts*, but falls short. The link between video games and literature is often evoked in order to build on the already well-developed structures of analysis of an older medium that can then (supposedly) be reasonably applied to the new. Sheldon (2004) located game narrative entirely within the story structures of films and novels; story elements are key, less so the medium. Likewise, the intertexuality of titles like *Star Wars* in game, text, and film supports the possibility of cross-media analysis,[9] though the quite different affordances of each medium should be considered. The distinct affordances of interactive digital media are most obvious in terms of agentive choice in video game play. Narrative takes on new forms with the addition of interactivity. Technology changes stories by making the reader an *interactor* with direct influence on the experience of *reading*.

Murray (1998) recognized that new media grow out of past traditions of art and storytelling[10] and explained that during the late 20th century (at the time of her writing), "in the incunabular days of the narrative computer, we can see how twentieth-century novels, films, and plays have been steadily pushing against the boundaries of linear storytelling" (p. 29). Electronic games are afforded some narrative similarity in Murray's text, though she does not consider *shoot-em up* or puzzle games. Murray (1998) argued that games "hold the potential for more powerful moments of revelation than they currently make use of" and points to the example of *Myst* (1993)[11] as one of the few games to incorporate a dramatic element (p. 54).

Figure 4.2 Screenshot of *Myst*. Myst [Video game]. (1993). Eugene, OR: Brøderbund Software, Inc.

Murray (1998) suggested that story webs and hypertext fiction are more narratively expressive than computer/console video games. Murray was writing at a time when many technological aspects of modern interactive digital gaming were not yet present, such as haptic feedback in most controllers, motion-sensing console accessories, 3D televisions, and 60+ inch widescreen viewing of high-definition cinematic graphics in people's homes. These advances changed the interactive environment's potential for player agency in terms of one's virtual-physical sense of presence in the game as well as immersive narrative potential.

4.2 Non-linear Storytelling and Narrative Elements of Interactivity

The relationship between game narrative and literature is not without debate due to intrinsic differences between media forms; new media requires an increased level of participation from the reader/player. Zancanella, Hall, and Pence (2000) described computer games as literature through an approach to games, not as something "to be won or puzzles to be solved, but rather as complex texts that evoke lived-through experiences" (p. 89), which certainly neglects the intrinsic incentive process of game play. *Heavy Rain* (2010), for example, demonstrates lived-through experience as elements of everyday life becoming a part of the virtual experience.

Zancanella et al. (2000) used literary criticism to explore the interactive world of digital gaming and suggested an analysis in which the words *reader* and *player* are interchangeable. They exclude *beat-em up* games and investigate console titles, which rely on narrative that requires a minimum "understanding [of] particular situations, developing characters, and problem-solving" rather than engaging in combat,

Figure 4.3 Realism in everyday action. Heavy Rain [Video game]. (2010). Tokyo, Japan: Sony Interactive Entertainment.

though admittedly combat-oriented games may profit from such literary analysis as well (p. 89). The image in Figure 4.4 is a quintessential beat-em up video game, *Streets of Rage* (1991), provided here as a counter-point; the characters progress along side-scrolling environments.

This type of play begs the question: is the lack of required action beyond pushing buttons on a controller (and the lack of detailed narrative) a distraction from the realism of game play? It could be that the fighting visually represented on the screen is just as *real* as the character brushing his teeth on the screen in *Heavy Rain* (2010). Importantly, Zancanella et al. (2000) related their own experiences and analyses of playing games and reported that once drawn into the story world of the game, they "each experienced thoughts and emotions evoked by the interplay of the text with [their] own personal backgrounds and understandings…[and] were immersed in an alternate reality that is the hallmark of a literary experience" (p. 99). My own experiences with interactive digital gaming mirror this belief, which aided in building rapport with interview participants and analyzing responses according to shared knowledge of what this form of play *feels* like. To write critically about interactive computer games (as a form of literature, art, or any other categorization), one must have played.[12]

Zancanella et al. (2000) suggested that because console game narratives are not simply a linear recounting of chronological events, they should be viewed as a mosaic, "more circular and recursive than print narratives have traditionally been," but not to an extent beyond that

Figure 4.4 Screenshot of *Streets of Rage*. Streets of Rage [Video game]. (1991). Tokyo, Japan: Sega.

of writers such as James Joyce, William Faulkner, or Toni Morrison who experimented with narrative in similar ways in strictly text-based media (p. 99). This perspective is easily contested, however. The narrative windings of text-based media can never hope to reach the levels of complexity possible with the help of computer hardware systems of data management and immersive visual data on a screen. Additionally, many games have quite linear narratives that include unique moments of game play in the midst of the narrative progression that require players to solve puzzles, navigate the game space, and defeat enemies as necessary to get to the next pre-determined narrative point.

The primary difference between traditional literature and computer games *as* literature is player/reader agency. When reading a book or watching a film, one might identify (relate to one's own lived experiences) with a character, but there is no sense of power or control over the direction that character takes in the provided narrative. Computer-based narratives in games blur the line between author and reader with the "player actually authoring events within the rule-governed world of the game" (Zancanella et al., 2000, p. 100). This level of involvement fosters deeper learning and internalization of concepts shared through the player-authored narrative progression. Narratives of new media are unique due to this incorporation of and reliance on the player.

If video games are not literature in the strictest sense, then what are they? Aarseth suggested that Ryan's approach to games is that of a *metaphor* for literary structure and play in which she "investigates the 'interactive' structures of games and game-like virtual reality installations and artistic 3D experiments (e.g. Brenda Laurel et al.'s 1992 project *Placeholder*[13]) with a view to how these forms can potentially become successful media for narrative expression" (Ryan, 2004, p. 406). Such examples are limited to hyper-text or narrative games, such as *Myst* (1993), or experimental theatrical productions rather than modern games with the current conceptions of narrative structures in interactive digital media play. Ryan focused on analyses of virtual reality in terms of head-mounted displays and data gloves, which are more physically immersive than a modern game console but arguably limit interactive experience (although that is rapidly changing as well). A bulky VR apparatus shields the player from physical realities of the space he or she occupies (an empty room, a seat on a couch, etc.) Interactivity is also experienced by players of the Nintendo Wii, albeit in a different way, in *Wii Sports* (2006).

Despite the lack of fully encompassing virtual reality systems in home entertainment,[14] today's in-home game consoles are the closest, and certainly most ubiquitous, example of this type of virtual reality yet. Though usually mediated by a television screen rather than a visor, virtual experiences take on real meaning for players, and a so-called literary critique of that system of meaning-making is a useful step in building an interdisciplinary understanding of ergodic ontogenetic influences.

Figure 4.5 Screenshot of *Wii Sports*. Wii Sports [Video game]. (2006). Kyoto, Japan: Nintendo.

Ryan (2001) discussed human input required for computer games or simulations in which "the simulation becomes the life story of the user, or rather the story of one of the user's virtual lives…Every action taken by the user is an event in the virtual world"[15] (p. 64). A virtual reality system is not simply a non-narrated narrative; it is a complex system of possible alternative stories with near-infinite potentiality. Interactivity is a key component to the digital environment and depends entirely on a computer system's responsiveness to changes in coded narrative as a result of user input. Computer games, a category in which console games may be included, are "generally not played for sake of their plot but frequently rely on concrete narrative elements – characters, setting, action – to lure players into the game world" (Ryan, 2004, p. 333). This focus is shifting in modern games as high-quality graphics and game mechanics are becoming the rule rather than the exception, and narrative complexity is becoming a game asset in itself.

The metaphors of *text as game* and *game as literature* are bolstered as Ryan (2004) described a *richness* of narrative such that games "may be read narratively without being narratives in either a diegetic or a strict mimetic sense"; if digital media creates "new forms of narrativity" then this has less to do with semantics than "presentational strategies (that is, discourse) and, above all, pragmatic factors: new modes of user involvement; new types of interface; and new relations between the author (or, rather, system designer), the plot (or plots), and users" (p. 333). This form of narrative analysis moves away from prior claims that text-based traditional literature is no less complex than the workings of computer systems, but still simplifies computer-based narrative works.

Aarseth situated computer games entirely within the discipline of ludology and avoided a relation to literary discourse; games do not rely on the "criteria that normally apply to literary narrative: believable characters, well-constructed plot, or high-flying metaphysics. The enjoyment of players is, rather, a matter of feeling empowered, of engaging in competition, of finding clever new ways to beat the system" (Ryan, 2004, p. 333). Aarseth's analysis involved the direction of representation: if narrative is representation, then games are simulation.[16] Ryan (2004) defined a narrative text as one that "brings a world to the mind (setting) and populates it with intelligent agents (characters). These agents participate in actions and happenings (events, plots), which cause global changes in the narrative world" (p. 337). Digital media is defined in terms of its reactive/interactive nature, multiple sensory and semiotic channels, networking capabilities, volatile signs (the ability to be refreshed/rewritten), and modularity (autonomous parts that can be used in various ways) (Ryan, 2004). However, computer games evolved at an unprecedentedly rapid rate, and (according to Aarseth) a "cultural evolution is still very much taking place. ... To simply talk about 'games' or even 'digital games,' seems irresponsible: there are large and widening differences between game genres, gaming situations, and game technologies" (Ryan, 2004, p. 362).

Analyses of games *in medias res* (though restricted by a lack of complete knowledge of the story at any given moment) may provide more strategic and reflective analyses, but games are usually only analyzed after they are played. More-complete critiques of human-computer interactivity in digital entertainment forms may results from traditional analysis coupled with real-time/*in medias res* analysis of game-play experiences by both casual gamers and researchers alike.

Theorists must experience this interactive form of narrative firsthand and be fully aware of the medium as they are simultaneously immersed in the digital realm. "Video games don't attempt to hide informatics control; they flaunt it. Look to the auteur work of game designers like Hideo Kojima,[17] Yu Suzuki,[18] or Sid Meier[19]" in which the gamer is "learning, internalizing, and becoming intimate with a massive, multipart, global algorithm" (Galloway, 2006, p. 90). This learning process, and personal/individual involvement, is part of a game's allure and establishes a connection between play experiences and reality that ultimately leads to ergodic ontogeny.

Descriptions of narrative algorithms in games are distinct from ludology. Ludology, the study of games/play, intentionally ignores character and story. Games may take the form of a linear narrative structure with story arcs throughout and may take artistic directions from cinematic scenes in film to progress narrative elements, but unlike other media, video games "also have nonlinear narratives that must unfold in algorithmic form during gameplay...[and] deliver to the player the power relationships of informatics media firsthand, choreographed into a multivalent cluster of play activities" (Galloway, 2006, p. 92). Game analyses must interpret visual and linguistic signs but also focus on the action of games, the *doing* that the player participates in. Galloway (2006) described this as an interpretation of *polyvalent doing*, in which "one must interpret material action instead of keeping to the relatively safe haven of textual analysis" (p. 105). Narrative theory, alone, is not comprehensive enough to thoroughly analyze a game narrative experience that constantly shifts and changes according to user input.

4.3 Interview Data: Experiences of Narrative

The way players talk about their personal experiences of game narrative is telling: there is a difference between narrative that is prescribed (other media forms) and that which is discovered or at times self-determined through interactive digital play. Players describe interactive media experiences and their *use* of games as well as their reactions to narrative elements during game play in specific ways. Despite the presence of symbols of domination in much of their speech, participants made concerted efforts to distance themselves through their discourse from overt stereotypes of masculinity and aggression. Recall the example from Chapter 1 of Copper, a participant serving in the U.S. military in the Middle East at the time of his interview. He described his experience playing the video game *Double Dragon 2: The Revenge* (1989) on the Nintendo Entertainment System and reflected on narrative points that had particular meaning (or not) for him as a player.

Copper expressed dissatisfaction with the cultural expectation, steeped in Western literary narrative tradition,[20] that men will take up a violent pursuit to rescue or protect a woman. Russ (1972) argued that culture is not only male but western European. But what does this mean in terms of *available stories* for interactive entertainment and other media? As an active agent in the narrative structure, the moral and psychological components of games will arguably be more affective on the reader (in this case player) than in less integrative texts. We must maintain a social awareness of the myths that are culturally available or acceptable and what the results of these limited narratives might be on audiences. A lack of "workable myths" or "acceptable dramatizations… harms much more than art itself. We do not only choose or reject works of art on the basis of these myths; we interpret our own experience in terms of them" and "perceive what happens to us in the mythic terms our culture provides" (Russ, 1972, p. 209). This consideration is crucial to the exploration of identity in terms of interactive media. If only certain stories are being told or are available in the cultural imagination, then apparent limitations of the medium are part of a flaw in the overall social structure that must be considered in wide, contextual terms. The female (importantly *non-player*) character that Copper described in the game is positioned as weaker and in needing of rescue[21] (a traditional archetype of many stories of heroes). Copper (C)'s discourse is repeated here for reference:

1. C: Uh (.) Billy's girlfriend in Double Dragon 2 gets kidnapped (.)
2. C: or murdered (.) I forget which (1) …
3. C: And then he enlists the aid of his brother (.)
4. C: cuz you know, <u>that's</u> what you do…
5. C: I <u>mean</u>, su::re?
6. C: Why n::ot (.) What are friends for?

As noted in Chapter 1, the character of the girlfriend is basically inconsequential, and Copper mocks the plot structure of the game through use of sarcasm and hyperbole. By asking "what are friends for" (line 6), he removes this narrative from the strictly game-related realm and applies it to his own ideologies of friendship and support, again with a tone that implies his negative opinion of male hegemonic status and certain cultural narratives that go along with it. The roles of men in United States society are accepted and understood, internalized by the player, but not condoned through these linguistic devices (Cole, 2014).

Games can be an outlet for aggression and competition. Themes of protection and strength were prominent in discourse for all interview participants. When asked about his enjoyment of game story elements and narrative themes, George connected his response to his work as a police officer.

George's response:

1. G: Personally, I think that though lots of humans have become
2. G: kind of compla::cent over the years,
3. G: that deep down we still have this primal <u>urge</u> to go and hunt
4. G: believe it or not (laughs)
5. G: And this primal urge to <u>protect</u> (.)
6. G: And since that's not as obvious (.)
7. G: I mean when I was a police officer,
8. G: that was certainly a thing about me that I could foster.
9. G: But um, I think without these outlets for that (referencing games)
10. G: I think we'd have a few mo::re, I guess uh (1)
11. G: I think we'd have a lot more problems in the <u>real</u> world

His use of terms like "humans" (line 1) as opposed to *people* and "primal urge" (lines 3 and 5) position this personal opinion as less casual/conversational and more academic or scientific/biological. This implies that his assertion is a basic or objective argument supporting our cultural norms of masculinity and why they are easily followed. Drawn out speech on the word "complacent" (line 2) indicates a stress on this idea, and an extended emphasis to draw the listener in to his argument, almost asking "do you know what I mean?" through the elongation of the central vowel sound. Laughter[22] (line 4) and the suggestion that his ideas, despite the scientifically situated terminology already discussed, might be difficult to "believe" (also line 4) suggest that the speaker feels the interviewer may need convincing or may not already be in agreement. This phrase, "believe it or not" (line 4), implies that what he is saying may seem odd, but truly is the case. Lastly, the emphasis in volume and intonation on the words "protect" (line 5) and "real" (line 11) stress their importance to the speaker in conveying his overall message.

Most participants referenced a role of the protector or hero in their narrativized stories of childhood play and gender self-identification (Cole, 2013).[23] Heroic Protective Discourse (HPD) as developed by Dryden, Doherty, and Nicolson (2010) positions the hero beyond traditional conceptions of idealized masculinity in terms of independence and control and reconstitutes an idea of heroism that "took on the additional dimension foregrounding the motivation to 'protect'" (p. 193). It is not enough for men to save the day or rescue the princess; they must protect family and friends from dangers before they arise, often before they are old enough or strong enough to intervene. Men, in that case (ill-equipped and too young), must anticipate dangers and opportunities in order to make decisions on behalf of women and, potentially other, weaker men, an expectation that supports no sense of agency for women or anyone other than the heroic figure.

This cultural tendency is enacted in many interactive entertainment gaming scenarios. Even a classic character example such as Mario (in *Donkey Kong*, 1981) is tasked with rescuing a princess, a goal that is motivated by the implication that he should not have allowed her to be kidnapped in the first place and that it is his role to save her and correct the situation. "HPD refers to a set of interpretive resources and practices that normalize a form of masculine identity that combines physical strength and aggression with the motivation to use physical force in the service of protecting others" (Dryden et al., 2010, p. 194). Participants' discourse supported such themes in relation to play practices, professional interests, and daily understandings of gender identities and modes of interaction (Cole, 2014). HPD is clearly reflected in career choices in military or police roles—defined by their purpose of protecting others—which reflects the way some men view themselves in a social context according to the narrative trends with which they are most familiar.

Players reported a sense of catharsis in the mundane elements of play. Violent game narratives in interactive entertainment media, despite many hedging statements to the contrary, emerged as a consistent theme for all participants and ultimately related to experiences of violence in professional settings in the real world (Cole, 2013). Participants confirmed their enjoyment of these traditional narratives and only admitted to recognition of some connection between work and play after qualifying their statements extensively. For instance, when asked about the stress of his line of work, George (G) stated:

1. G: Especially if you had a <u>really</u> bad day, and uh (2)
2. G: I was a [state omitted] State Trooper for a while
3. G: and I was retired from that work
4. G: but ev::ery once in a while there would be someone
5. G: that you wish you could just go up to and hit (.)
6. G: with the butt of a rifle (laughs) (.)
7. G: and you could obviously <u>do</u> that in Halo
8. G: without any real consequences (laughing)
9. I: Right
10. G: //I think honestly (.) this is just my personal opinion
11. G: I have <u>n::o</u> statistics or anything to back it up (.)
12. G: but without some of these games
13. G: a lot more of us would be sociopaths (laughs)

Even though he had a potentially violent career path as a police officer, there were still rules by which to abide. Aggression, a purely emotional response, may not be enacted physically in reality. George hedges his assertion repeatedly with laughs (lines 6, 8, and 13) to connote that he would never actually hit someone with his rifle and to build empathy with the listener. George also includes numerous phrases of uncertainty regarding the link between the release of aggression in games and consequences of that release in reality such as "I honestly think" and "just my personal opinion" (line 10), which imply that he does not want to be held to specifics but does want to draw the listener in by promising an "honest" thought at the moment of his interruption (// in line 10). Another example is the phrase "no statistics or anything" (line 11). However, he ultimately shares a fundamental connection, stating "without some of these games" (line 12), between the restraint required of him at work despite the real tensions present there, and the release found in play with violent narratives or in-game experiences.

Though participants denied the idea that training might go on in entertainment or game scenarios, many did express similar emotional connections. The normative discourse of violence in males is evidenced repeatedly in terms of acceptable language use, activity, professional pursuits, and displays of emotion. In a linguistic analysis of men's talk about emotion, Walton, Coyle, and Lyons (2004) described being *upset* as an emotion that is only culturally acceptable for men if it is expressed through "anger and violence" (p. 407). Game play, then, could serve as an outlet for anger as well as other emotional responses while maintaining culturally acceptable expressions of masculinity.

Narrative analysts found that male respondents hesitate when asked about emotions such as fear and find that a "major similarity across [the] interviews was the silence that followed the question" about fear (Sandberg & Tollefsen, 2010, p. 9). Being afraid does not fit the traditional masculine narrative of protection and aggression.[24] For instance, Copper's discourse described part of a violent game narrative that disturbed him.

Copper's response:

1. C: Well, I'll tell ya (.) the uh (.)
2. C: and I have been a Call of Duty player
3. C: when Modern Warfare 1 came out, and the thing is...
4. C: there is a (.) uh, there's the control thing.
5. C: They actually took a moment, took the time to program it
6. C: so there is a scene where you're sneaking in the jungles of
7. C: Vietnam...
8. C: You come up, there's this, um (.) Vietcong in the boat...
9. C: And you come up and you have to take the joystick
10. C: and move it this way, like move it (.) circle it around.
11. C: And you come up out of the water and slit the guys throat
12. C: in the most unbelievably unpleasantly graphic
13. C: way possible (2)
14. C: And uh (1.5) I found that really unpleasant

This description has hesitation in the form of "uh" and "um" four times, seven distinct pauses, and disjointed sentence structures that imply discomfort with the topic at hand. These are also indicators of the speaker's lack of clarity of thought in trying to express an emotional reaction of this sort. Detail is provided in terms of the game-play and what the narrative entails, but the only information given about his personal emotional response to that content (other than what is implied through the irregularity of his speech) is the repetition of the word "unpleasant" in lines 12 and 14, rather than upsetting, frightening, disturbing, troubling, or other potentially more emotionally evocative adjectives.

The narrative and ludic elements of this section of the game were distractingly realistic or reminiscent of an experience outside the game world, taking the player outside of the distraction that was pleasingly thoughtless while fully engaging and calling attention to the negative aspects of such feelings in reality. Details about game mechanics, such the "program" (line 5) and the use of a "joy stick" (line 9), distance the speaker from an emotional connection and express the importance of physical interaction with the interactive narrative through such devices. The story does not proceed without player action, physically moving the joy stick, and implicating oneself in the outcome of this narrative moment.

4.4 Divergent Pathways and Potentialities

Narrative diversity influences programming potentials for player input and character choice. Agency as the distinguishing factor in interactive digital media facilitates a deeper connection with narrative points, broadening the influence of traditional storytelling techniques, fables, and heroic story arcs. Some of the most successful game franchises[25] are those with immersive story elements reminiscent of film or miniseries that engage the player while maintaining a sense of individual experience and choice (agency) and demonstrate the potential for divergent, or at least open, paths in game play.

A linear plot is but one of many ways to engage players who are literate in interactive digital gaming. Many games pride themselves on establishing a sense of openness in the virtual world, and an incentivized goal structure through which to progress—even if that progression is at one's own pace and in what might feel like randomized order. Linear game play is still common, however, with varying levels of narrative detail. Examples of linear game storytelling include the *Halo* series (2001–2017) and *Uncharted* (2007–2016), among many others. There is no difference in the story (though specific actions are unique to each experience) or outcome of the successfully complete game regardless of the player. The overarching story remains static while methods of completion may vary. Each player can determine how best to accomplish short-term goals between narrative moments, but after the completion of these sections, the story continues as it would regardless of the specific way the goal was reached.

Narrative elements of beat-em up/shoot-em up games are similar in that the story will proceed in a set fashion with little if any variety. The ludic elements of game play (learning the moves, codes, and systems of the game as if deciphering a puzzle) are the primary incentives for this type of play.[26] Almost all fighting games, despite asserting a *story mode* option, fall into this category as well. Players of *Mortal Kombat* (1992), *Street Fighter* (1987), or *Dead or Alive* (1996) are all similarly focused on button mashing and short-term competition for action-based entertainment purposes with a loose narrative structure.

Many fighting games include brief verbal phrases from characters that are not established elsewhere in a narrative and serve simply to introduce the characters visually and prepare the player for action. The term *story mode* for such games is misleading.

The *Silent Hill* (1999–2011) and *Castlevania* (1986–2013) series are early console gaming examples that provided multiple endings depending on how the player completed certain parts of the game. However, this type of narrative differentiation is not chosen. It relies on the actions of the player during game play. For the game *Silent Hill*,[27] the ending depends on the order and thoroughness of the player's exploration of the

Figure 4.6 Screenshot of *Dead or Alive 4*. Dead or Alive 4 [Video game]. (2005). Tokyo, Japan: Tecmo.

town and actions within it. *Castlevania* titles often end differently depending on which items the player found during the course of the game. Another example is *Pikmin* (2001), which incorporates a timed element; the player completes the game after successfully rebuilding his ship in the allotted minutes or fails at that mission, but the game ends either way.

The most common means of sharing the story of a game with the player is through expositional *cut-scenes*. An example of extensive narrative content in cut-scene format can be found in the *Metal Gear* series of video games in which Hideo Kojima's intricate web of political commentary is woven skillfully between game play experiences of espionage action. Cut-scenes, the non-playable scenes between playable experiences in video games, are often cinematic in nature—mirroring a scene in a film to provide the player with information integral to understanding the next steps of the game. Games that rely heavily on cut-scenes to entertain players often feel more like movies than they do like the traditional concept of video games. Examples of this type of narrative structure include games such as the *Final Fantasy* series (1987–2017), *Uncharted* (2007–2016), and *Red Dead Redemption* (2010).

The incentive in this type of game is to continue the story and successfully navigate a character through the given narrative. Cut-scenes sometimes include game-play elements such as Quicktime events to maintain a player's attention and require feedback in order to proceed with the story, such as the need to jump out of the way of harmful objects or enemies in *Resident Evil* (1996) or the level of involvement at most moments of play during *Shenmue* (1999), a unique play experience with realistic pacing, or *God of War* (2005). A final distinction in plot and incentives in these narrative-driven games is whether or not cut-scenes take place in-engine (like *Red Dead Redemption*, *Metal Gear*, or *Grand Theft Auto* (GTA)) or are pre-rendered (*Silent Hill*, *Resident Evil*, or *Final Fantasy*). Though pre-rendered graphics are often visually superior, the shift in visual representation may cause a rift in the *flow* of play during these moments. As graphics improved, however, the need for pre-rendered cut-scenes diminished, and they are now used more often for artistic effect.[28]

The complex understanding of new media necessary to fully appreciate and engage with interactive digital entertainment forms is a new kind of literacy resulting in new levels of ergodic ontogeny. Many recent games take advantage of the increasingly more-literate/electrate population and pursue immersive qualities of flexible storytelling that provide detailed and diverse narrative options. Emergent game play, as possible in the *GTA* and *Elder Scrolls* (1994–2015) series and other sandbox games,[29] provides so many diverse in-game experiences that players can ignore the principle narrative if they choose.

Many games have small tasks/quests that must be accomplished, either to achieve a level of experience, gain items, etc., before continuing with the primary story, but these are usually cursory goals that would lose allure in short order. Narrative is an essential element of many games, though cut-scenes are not always necessary. Some examples of enacted narrative are *Demon Souls* (2009) and *Dark Souls* (2011), in which the player cannot pause the game, or games like *Portal* (2007) in which the entire narrative is played through (no cut-scenes at all).

The importance of game narrative is clear in the *Mass Effect* (2007–2017) series, which continues the storyline across three games, each building from the choices the player made in the previous games. *Mass Effect* games allow the player to continue through a singular timeline, unlike games with repeated characters (like Mario or Donkey Kong) or shared

Figure 4.7 Sandbox Games. Grand Theft Auto V [Video game]. (2013). New York, NY: Take-Two Interactive.

universes (like *Zelda* or *Castlevania*).[30] *Mass Effect* games continue their narrative arc and use established forms of exposition through a mixture of enacted and cinematic in-engine cut-scenes. This type of game, similar to the *Fable* series (2004–2014), *Knights of the Old Republic* (2003–2015) (KOTOR), and *Jade Empire* (2005), is distinguished by the incorporation of conscious decision-making on the part of the player regarding how story and game play options progress. Usually broken down simplistically as either *good* or *bad* characters, again keeping with the most basic and traditional aspects of narrative, these games rely on story to supplement game play, keeping players engaged at each level. They also include multiple endings and variations in narrative depending on decisions of the player, leading to increased levels of agency. Not only is the player responding to the system, providing input and feedback to the coding of the game itself, he or she is also made acutely aware of the path not taken through the inclusion of either dialogue or enacted moments with overt decision-making.

Players usually navigate game worlds via the movement of avatars or first-person points of view through virtual space. This movement is dictated by tangible/physical interaction with a controller or sensor and according to the narrative choices made through dialogue responses that are left up to the player. Agency, in terms of dialogue choices, highlights the path not taken, the conversation avoided, and the potential for players to feel they are making their own way through game play. Dialogue interactions (dialogue trees) draw on expectations established in text-based games in which the player is given a list of choices for response. *Mass Effect*, for example, uses *dialogue trees* through which the player can choose narrative/speech that is oriented in a generalized hierarchy. Usually, if the player chooses the top dialogue option, it will reflect more kind, generous, or understanding speech options (resulting in points toward being a morally *good* character). Choosing the lower option accomplishes the opposite goal.

Figure 4.8 Dialogue trees with QR Code. Mass Effect 3 [Video game]. (2012). Edmonton, Canada: Bioware. https://vimeo.com/185082703.

Mass Effect games contain dialogue trees through which the character can simply move the story along (middle/highlighted option), ask for more information and show interest in the non-player character (top option), or dismiss the situation while exhibiting what could be interpreted as a short-temper or gruff attitude (bottom option). Placing the player in a position to choose narrative progression—when it takes place, what is said (within the limits provided), and which of the non-player characters the player addresses—heightens ergodic identification and ultimately results in increased ergodic ontogeny. The player chooses, to a greater extent than available ever before, his or her own story: an act that makes him or her acutely aware of the options that were not chosen and the narrative elements that can only be imagined as possible alternatives to the direction in which he or she proceeds.

Games like *Silent Hill* provide alternate endings depending on which parts of the game are successfully completed and depending on the methods of completion. This is different from games like *Mass Effect*, *Fable*, and *KOTOR* in that the player is less aware of the path not taken, continuing along through a seamless narrative structure more-or-less unaware of narrative alternatives. In games like the *Mass Effect* series,[31] however, dialogue trees are ever present and a crucial aspect of game play (providing *paragon* or *renegade* points, another incentive process depending on the type of character desired).

Juxtaposed characters visually representing light/dark characters from *Knights of the Old Republic*, for example, have obvious cues (color, posture, indicator bar, status settings) that reflect the number of points accumulated by the player toward either the light or dark side of the Force, a system with direct metaphorical implications to personal morality and character.

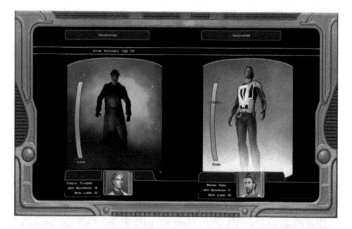

Figure 4.9 Screenshot of *Knights of the Old Republic*. Star Wars: Knights of the Old Republic [Video game]. (2012). Edmonton, Canada: Bioware.

Immersion in the virtual play environment through which narrative is revealed and experienced is discussed in detail in the next chapter. This concept, as related to new forms of visual and ergodic literacy/electracy, helps explain how players understand in-game realities and the ways in which digital graphics alter perceptions. One of the most obvious and commonly discussed contributions to immersion in many video games is that of character creation (a playable character created, within the limits of available graphic options, by the player rather than by the game developer).

Ergodic ontogeny, resultant self-identification and ideological leanings, is supported by various disciplines that explore the influence of technology on the *self*. Thomas (2008) explained that early "landmark studies often emphasized participant experience of anonymity affording freedom to 'try on' new identities...more recent ethnographic studies and linguistic studies...questioned the notion that anonymity equates to the total freedom and uninhibited ability to do and be anybody or anything" (p. 672–73). The reality of electronic media communication is less freeing than originally imagined. Players may choose to play as predetermined characters or create personalized representations that are very much like themselves (neglecting an option to try on new personas).

Knowledge of technologically mediated worlds influences interactions in game experiences and in reality. For instance, physically or socially determined roles, such as gender, can be challenged in play. As Dines and Humez (2011) explained, "users have the agency to create the gender roles and the sexual experiences that they want" (p. 571), and "this agency is theorized from a liberatory perspective that sees cyberspace as a unique social arena in which traditional gender roles...[are] transgressed" (p. 572). However, there are "those who use their agency to reproduce the traditional roles and norms found in real life" (Dines & Humez, 2011, p. 572). Gender is but one element of identification that can be blurred, embraced, or ignored through virtual game play experiences. Even if a player creates a character entirely different from him/herself, the reasons for decisions made during play and the player's relationship to that character are still dictated by the influences that produced the individual in reality.[32]

Character creation is embraced for purposes of changing one's expression of self and in order to add new levels of personalization and connection to game play experiences by accurately recreating the physical self. Whether forming an accurate recreation of oneself or the total opposite, the more detailed the graphical interface options for character creation, the better. The level of detail possible with character creators increases with each new console generation.

A sense of agency, personal active involvement in the narrative, increases if the character enacting story moments on screen is either physically similar[33] to the player or if the player feels invested in the

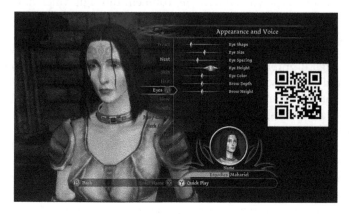

Figure 4.10 Character creation with QR Code. Dragon Age: Origins [Video game]. (2009). Redwood City, CA: Electronic Arts. https://vimeo.com/185107417.

character more than a stock visual because of his or her involvement in its inception (Williams, Martins, Consalvo, & Ivory, 2009).[34] Other immersive elements of interactive digital play include being able to make team/group members who look like and are named after real friends, as is possible in games like *XCom* (2012–2016) or *Madden NFL* (1988–2016) and other sports games. This enhances the play experience through increased (providing a connection to reality) or decreased (knowledge of people in real life and the dissonance between that reality and their in-game personas) immersion. Character creation also results in some hindrances to character development and narrative involvement. If a game has a stock character with specific attributes set by the developer, then that character can be given a backstory, name, and other defined character elements. If a game permits character creation, then some aspects of that character must be necessarily vague, or at least creatively avoided, in order to work with any traits the player chooses, thus altering the storytelling abilities of developers.

4.5 Experiential Narrative Forms

Increased engagement of the player through feelings of agency in play is the primary goal of strong narrative and character arcs in games. Interactive entertainment, especially games with clearly delineated, if divergent (depending on the player) narrative structures, is bound to the options available through the coding of the game and the possible levels of character creation and ergodic identification with a given avatar. The narrative, character, and choice (agency) provided in virtual play experiences, limited as they are, influence players and reinforce the cultural norms expressed through the particular games that are played.

The player is paramount. The complex interactions between characters and players, as well as the content of game worlds' narratives (both enacted and cinematic cut-scenes), are compared to past media forms. Despite debate regarding the importance of narrative and narrative theory to video game studies, "most scholars and industry commentators agree that, at their heart, video games are experiential and are concerned with doing" (Newman, 2009, p. 511). Video games are participatory and active, which requires analysis of text and of the narrative unfolding within play experiences. Games must be defined as *interactive,* "even if this means erroneously attributing 'passivity' to media such as television, film, literature, and so on" (Newman, 2009, p. 511). Players' contribution to play is the distinguishing factor and must be the starting point of any thorough analysis of interactive virtual play.

The process of ergodic ontogeny (individual personal development incorporating stimuli/influences of the ludic and narrative elements of interactive media play environments) requires that we keep in mind the complexity of the player/character relationship at "the level of simulation, rules, and systems" (Newman, 2009, p. 511). Contrary to Newman, ergodic ontogeny requires an equal level of import be deemed to players' connections to specific or identifiable characters. Even the discourse of game hardware, such as *controllers* ("the switches and buttons of joysticks, pads, paddles, or even bongos and guitars"), emphasizes the "power of the player to direct and dictate the action and may help to place them at the center of this experience" (Newman, 2009, p. 511). Player experiences further distance computer/console gaming from other media, and aid in deepening the connection between player, system, and narrative.

Video games as a form of interactive television, a description that could only be applied on the most superficial level, sits in "stark contrast to the ways in which many players describe their play experiences that are not discussed in terms of vicarious pleasure or the remote control of characters but rather are recounted as first-hand experiences and discussed in the first-person" (Newman, 2009, p. 512). Despite common third-person perspectives in video games themselves, the goals of game characters are internalized and expressed as being met personally by the player, not as the character viewed on screen.

If play is "recounted in the first person [then]…rather than being an act of control, video game play is an act of performance that sees the video game 'character' reconfigured as a 'cursor" (Newman, 2009, p. 512). This relates to player expectation and agency in terms of interface transparency and designers' attempts at (potentially unnecessary) levels of realism. Interactive digital games are not simply visual representations on a screen, they are "kinesthetic and visceral and the interface, far from being a potential barrier to immersion or presence, is just one of the tools at the disposal of the designer in sculpting the emotional and experiential journey" (Newman, 2009, p. 516). Players expect to learn games' functions and response systems. This does not detract from the flow of the play experience as they progress through multi-modal narratives as the characters they perform.

The next chapter will address the role of the player even more directly through concepts of personal identification and identity construction. The nature of digital environments and their levels of immersion, growing societal familiarity with digital alter-egos, potentially evocative interactions with non-player characters, and levels of believability in virtual reality scenarios will be explored in terms of individual ideology construction and self-identification. Connections between personal conceptions of gender identity and experiences of video game play are supported through interview data regarding expressions of masculinity in a U.S. cultural context.

Notes

1 Hazel (2008) pointed out that "because our experiences are time dependent and because our basic memory encoding system is episodic it seems inevitable that our fundamental mode of expression should be time sensitive, i.e. narrativized" (p. 203).

2 Though Hazel's work is focused in this instance on interactive learning environments and pedagogical implications, the descriptions of narrative are easily transferred to interactive entertainment media and help frame the importance of narrative in the study of the communication and epistemology of this type of play.

3 The structure of language itself is "instrumental in moderating traumatic distress...as the constraints of narrative may supply cognitive tools suitable for 'the emotional work of traumatic assimilation'" (Sandberg & Tollefsen, 2010, p. 3).

4 Sandberg and Tollefson (2010) provided an approach to narrative analysis of discourse that incorporated a self-reflexive turn in storytelling. Their article situated talk about fear in terms of public space. Space is, like time, often overlooked as arbitrary to research findings, but this is not the case and can certainly not be considered an innocent oversight within digital virtual realms. The method of linking meaning to space was employed by geographers Sandberg and Tollefson, which ties emotion and language to place, adding an important layer of analysis and consideration to social research and applying their technique across disciplines as a means of connecting layers of meaning to broader social relations.

5 The fear-risk paradox is the idea that those least victimized by violent crime are also the most fearful. Smith and Torstensson (1997) attributed this paradox to the hidden victimization of women, a greater tendency for women to recall previous fearful experiences, the real or socially constructed sense of vulnerability of women, and the discounting/dismissal of male fear.

6 Martha Nussbaum's *Cultivating Humanity* (1997) argued that narrative imagination is necessary for the rational aspects of democratic citizenship and for the emotional and sympathetic aspects as well.

7 Von Wright (2002) stated that "to change their habits and to actually make different choices, [people] need to be confronted with their habits and encouraged

to question them and to restate their moral values. Developing logical reasoning and critical argumentation is not, however, enough" (p. 409).

8 Recall Ulmer (2002).

9 See James Newman and Iain Simons' chapter in *New Narratives: Stories and Storytelling in the Digital Age* (Page & Thomas, 2011).

10 She traced multiform stories including attempts at placing the audience in a more active, less prescribed, role. The highly involved level of story in such texts is related to 3D films and amusement park rides that take participants on a journey according to a particular narrative.

11 In *Myst* (1993), a computer/PC game, the player (first person point-of-view) is on an island with no knowledge of how or why he or she is there. Through exploration of the surroundings and creative connections between found objects, artifacts, and interaction points, the player navigates the game world and eventually reveals the story.

12 For details of my positionality as a gamer, see Chapter 6.

13 Information about Laurel's multi-person narrative project can be found here: http://www.tauzero.com/Brenda_Laurel/Placeholder/Placeholder. html. A video documentary is also available - http://vimeo.com/27344103.

14 PlayStation VR, Google Glass, and Oculus Rift are recent exceptions.

15 "The sum of these events may not present proper dramatic form – an Aristotelian rise and fall of tension – but because all events involve the same participant they automatically satisfy the looser pattern of the epic or serial (episodic) narrative" (Ryan, 2001, p. 64).

16 Aarseth quotes Ragnild Tronstad on narrative to describe the ways in which "its illocutionary mode is the constative, since its purpose is to tell us what happened" whereas simulation is "oriented forward, and its illocutionary mode is the performative" (Ryan, 2004, p. 333). Ryan (2004) suggested that a "retrospective availability of meaning [in games] is sufficient to ascribe narrativity" (p. 334) though Aarseth would argue that at such a point the game would no longer be a simulation (no longer active in retrospect since a game must be played).

17 Kojima is best known for the *Metal Gear* game franchise (1987–2015).

18 Suzuki is a prolific designer for Sega and creator of games such as *Hang-On* (1985), *VirtuaFighter* (1993), and *Shenmue* (1999).

19 Meier is known for the *Civilization* series (1991–2015).

20 As Russ (1972) explained, if the *narrative mode* "concerns itself with *events* connected by the *chronological order* in which they occur, and the *dramatic mode* with *voluntary human actions* which are connected both by *chronology and causation*, then the principle of construction...[called] *lyric* consists of the *organization of discrete elements* (images, events, scenes, passages, words, what-have-you) *around an unspoken thematic or emotional center*" (p. 207).

21 Damsels in distress or princess characters are terms associated with knighthood and the age of chivalry or male-dominant romantic love in Western tradition.

22 Beach (2000) suggested that "inviting collaborations are apparent and embedded within and across the following actions" such as "invoking shared knowledge" and "mocking, laughing, and crude humor" (p. 383).

23 Espinosa and Clemente (2013) explored the connection between self and character and explained that "the effects of media on behavior are related to the socialization pattern and role-taking opportunities [games] offer" (p. 68). Although "the connection between media irrespective of content and antisocial behavior" is unresolved, "there is some evidence that the global amount of time spent watching television and using video games is related to

verbal and physical aggression"; the "time displacement hypothesis argues that media use takes time away from other social activities and may have an influence on cognitive development" (Espinosa & Clemente, 2013, p. 69). Time displacement and social incompetence theories suggest that studies should focus on "cognitive variables related to the children and adolescents' social perspective" (Espinosa & Clemente, 2013, p. 70). Despite potential connections between video game play and increased antisocial behavior, cognitive variables (self-transcendence and self-oriented perspectives) mediate this relationship in meaningful ways.

24 The most acceptable form of masculine emotional expression in Western culture is that of anger. Brown (1998) discussed limitations on women's expression of anger and explained forms of white middle-class psychological difficulty with this feeling that anger is often re- appropriated (as hysteria or rage) by dominant society and inherently tied to self-respect, a quality that makes subordination of a group more difficult if not impossible. As a result, girls' anger becomes increasingly less direct. Brown argued that "girls' increased anger and assertiveness at [age] eleven and twelve reflects their emerging comprehension of the culture they are about to enter and their place as young women in it" (p. 15). These expressions manifest differently depending on norms taught while growing up, often determined by class, culture, and race. Young males experience a similar awakening to their gender-specific roles in culture, but expressions of anger, strength, and aggression are condoned and fostered as they enter positions of social dominance.

25 The economic influence and proliferation of interactive digital game play is relevant to game story types (*Elder Scrolls, Sims, GTA,* or *WoW)* that sell the best.

26 Examples of this type of game include many early titles with little narrative flexibility such as *Ninja Gaiden* (1988), *Double Dragon* (1989), *Battle Toads* (1991), *Streets of Rage* (1991), and examples from the Xbox Live arcade like *Castle Crashers* (2008).

27 User-generated walk-throughs are available at gamefaq.com. The various endings and the required items are listed at http://www.gamefaqs.com/ps/198641-silent-hill/faqs/4183.

28 Some games have animated cut-scenes, like *Catherine* (2011) that has high quality visuals that add to the artistic value of the game or *Mirror's Edge* (2008), which though extremely innovative in terms of game play and perspective has cut-scene graphics that are arguably less effective.

29 Open-world games with high levels of player influence allowing for emergent game play.

30 It is important to note again that the focus here is on single-player console games. Online interaction (Xbox Live or Playstation Network) or multiplayer scenarios change the narrative options, number of players informing the direction of play, and the narration of play moments (when online talk is included). This, therefore, shifts the type of new media literacy required for game play. MMORPGs (massively multiplayer online role-playing games) communicative forms are different as well.

31 Another example is *The Walking Dead* (2012) in which decisions that lead to divergent paths are the primary elements of game play.

32 Dines and Humez (2011) explained that "theorizing from Foucault and Butler, a fundamental problem with the liberatory perspective emerges. Although the disciplining of gender and sexuality may be exercised on the body, this discipline produces a sexual subject who imagines itself independent of the body. Liberating this subject from the body via cyberspace does

not necessarily mean that this subject escapes the influential disciplinary practices that produced its identity" (p. 573).

33 This is not quite like Carr's (2006) concept of ergodic identification. She reported players expressing game experiences in terms of themselves versus the characters they are playing as, for instance, "I" entered the cave, but "she died" (when the obstacle was not overcome inside the cave). Other reports (including Cole, 2013) indicate that characters are chosen based on physical characteristics that are physically attractive to the player (female form, for instance) rather than representative of the self.

34 A more detailed discussion of Williams et al. (2009) is included in Chapter 6 regarding limited identities for unexpected players.

References

Aarseth, E. J. (1997). *Cybertext: Perspectives on ergodic literature.* Baltimore, MD: Johns Hopkins University Press.

Barthes, R. (1977). Image, music, text. In S. Heath (Ed.), *The photographic message* (p. 15–31). New York, NY: Hill.

Beach, W. (2000). Inviting collaborations in stories about a woman. *Language in Society, 29,* 379–407.

Brown, L. M. (1998). *Raising their voices: The politics of girls' anger.* Cambridge, MA: Harvard University Press.

Bruner, J. S. (2003). *Making stories: Law, literature, life.* Cambridge, MA: Harvard University Press.

Carr, D. (2006). *Computer games: Text, narrative and play.* Cambridge, UK: Polity.

Cole, S. (2013). Discourses of masculinity: Culture, identity and violence. In D. Boswell, R. O'Shea and E. Tzadik (Eds.), *Interculturalism, meaning and identity* (p. 153–164). Oxford, UK: Inter-Disciplinary Press.

Cole, S. (2014). Gender identity construction through talk about video games. Special issue: New works on electronic literature and cyberculture. *CLC Web: Comparative Literature and Culture, 15*(16.5). Retrieved from http://dx.doi.org/10.7771/1481-4374.2487.

Dines, G., & Humez, J. M. (2011). *Gender, race, and class in media: A critical reader.* Thousand Oaks, CA: Sage Publications.

Dryden, C., Doherty, K., & Nicolson, P. (2010). Accounting for the hero: A critical psycho-discursive approach to children's experience of domestic violence and the construction of masculinities. *British Journal of Social Psychology, 49*(1), 189–205.

Espinosa, P., & Clemente, M. (2013). Self-transcendence and self-oriented perspective as \ mediators between video game playing and aggressive behaviour in teenagers. *Journal of Community & Applied Social Psychology, 23*(1), 68–80.

Galloway, A. R. (2006). *Gaming: Essays on algorithmic culture.* Minneapolis, MN: University of Minnesota Press.

Hazel, P. (2008). Toward a narrative pedagogy for interactive learning environments. *Interactive Learning Environments, 16*(3), 199–213.

Labov, W., & Waletzky, J. (1967). Narrative analysis: Oral versions of personal narratives. In J. Helm (Ed.), *Essays on the verbal and visual arts: Proceedings* of the 1966 annual spring meeting of the American Ethnological Society (p. 12–44). Seattle: University of Washington Press.

McGonigal, J. (2015). *Superbetter: A revolutionary approach to getting stronger, happier, braver, and more resilient – powered by the science of games.* New York, NY: Penguin Press.

Murray, J. H. (1998). *Hamlet on the holodeck: The future of narrative in cyberspace.* Cambridge, MA: The MIT Press.

Newman, J. (2009). Playing the system: Video games/players/characters. *Semiotica, 173*(1–4), 509–524. doi:10.1515/SEMI.2009.024.

Nussbaum, M. C. (1997). *Cultivating humanity: A classical defense of reform in liberal education.* Cambridge, MA: Harvard University Press.

Page, R., & Thomas, B. (2011). *New narratives: Stories and storytelling in the digital age.* Lincoln, NE: University of Nebraska Press.

Russ, J. (1972). What can a heroine do? Or why women can't write. In. S. Koppelman (Ed.), *Images of women in fiction: Feminist perspectives* (p. 3–20). Bowling Green, OH: Bowling Green University Popular Press.

Ryan, M.-L. (2001). *Narrative as virtual reality: Immersion and interactivity in literature and electronic media.* Baltimore, MD: Johns Hopkins University Press.

Ryan, M.-L. (Ed.). (2004). *Narrative across media: The languages of storytelling.* Lincoln, NE: University of Nebraska Press.

Sandberg, L., & Tollefsen, A. (2010). Talking about fear of violence in public space: Female and male narratives about threatening situations in Umeå, Sweden. *Social & Cultural Geography, 11*(1), 1–15.

Sheldon, L. (2004). *Character development and storytelling for games.* Boston, MA: Cengage Learning.

Smith, W., & Torstensson, M. (1997). Gender differences in risk perception and neutralizing fear of crime: Toward resolving the paradoxes. *British Journal of Criminology, 37*(4), 608–634.

Thomas, A. (2008). Community, culture and citizenship in cyberspace. In J. Coiro, M. Knobel, C. Lankshear, & D. Leu, *Handbook of research on new literacies* (p. 671–698). New York, NY: Routledge.

Ulmer, G. L. (2002). *Internet invention: From literacy to electracy.* London, UK: Longman.

Von Wright, M. (2002). Narrative imagination and taking the perspective of others. *Studies in Philosophy and Education, 21*(4), 407–416.

Walton, C., Coyle, A., & Lyons, E. (2004). Death and football: An analysis of men's talk about emotions. *British Journal of Social Psychology, 43*(3), 401–416.

Williams, D., Martins, N., Consalvo, M., & Ivory, J. D. (2009). The virtual census: Representations of gender, race and age in video games. *New Media & Society, 11*(5), 815–834.

Zancanella, D., Hall, L., & Pence, P. (2000). Computer games as literature. In A. Goodwyn (Ed.), *English in the digital age: Information and communications technology (ICT) and the teaching of English* (p. 87–102). New York, NY: Cassell.

5 Ideology and Self-Identification

I'd like to be the person who keeps trying to say, and keeps trying to convince himself, that he was not a big first-person shooter gamer, but the reality is...

—George

5.1 Identity and Ideology: Discourse, Gender, and Character Connections

The ways players talk about their experiences of interactive digital play reflect the identity and ideological constructs of those individuals. Van Dijk (2006) suggested ways in which discourse influences and reflects ideological identification,[1] and defined ideologies as belief systems that are socially shared by group members; these belief systems are fundamental, core, or axiomatic and are gradually gained and lost over time through discourse. Within game narratives, players perform actions that align with ideologies (belief systems) through agentive action in interactive digital games, a process that leads to ergodic ontogenesis. Terms as elusive as *ideology* and *belief* can sometimes be best understood in terms of what they are not. Van Dijk (2006) explained that ideologies are *not* personal beliefs and are not necessarily negative; ideologies might define a belief system of resistance, domination, or legitimate dominance. Ideologies do *not* express false consciousness and are not themselves discourses or social practices (these express ideology); they can be defined as widely shared beliefs or ideas that have been constructed and disseminated by the powerful (in this case, the entertainment industry or game programmer, more specifically, who has personal interests and goals for the often traditional narrative and ludic elements chosen for inclusion in games). Ideological constructions reflect experiences of game creators and function for their benefit (Rosenblum & Travis, 2008). Ideologies are the socio-cognitive interfaces between the social structures of a group and their discourses and other social practices (Van Dijk, 2006).[2]

Ideological discourse analysis does not suggest that words, phrases, topics, or intonations are ideologically biased, only their specific use in communicative acts. To determine ideological implications of discourse, researchers must know the text (co-text) and context: who is speaking, to whom, when, and with what intention. Van Dijk (2006) stressed that discourse accomplishes many things beyond the expression or reproduction of ideologies and in/out group identification[3] and distinguished between personal beliefs of individuals and group ideologies that lead (only sometimes) to group knowledge. Ultimately, ideologies apply only to groups that position themselves in relation to other groups, as the Other, with positive self-presentation and negative other-presentation (Van Dijk, 2006). Studying players' discourses of game play experiences provides a window into potential ideological influences of interactive digital media when applied in this context.

Identity construction is similarly complicated. Duggan (1993) described identity construction as a historical "process of contested narration, a process in which contrasting 'stories' of the self or others – stories of difference – are told, appropriated, and retold as stories of location in the social world of structured inequalities" (p. 361). Identity is inherently linked to historical location within social structures. Especially during social transformations, "stories of identity are never static, monolithic, or politically innocent. By situating people within shifting structures of social power and inequality, they become contested sources of authority and legitimation" (Duggan, 1993, p. 361). Ergodic ontogeny and self-representation are historically situated and dependent on a number of external factors. The process of ergodic ontogeny is reflective of the experiences that shape the understandings of the player and his or her relationship to virtual-life moments within a game.

The predominance of male characters and masculine themes in many video games necessitates a discussion of gender self-identification of players as well as the gendered representations within interactive media content. The dominant cultural representation of masculinity in the United States, and most western societies, involves the "concealment of emotions that might imply vulnerability or dependency although it permits the expression of emotions such as anger" (Walton, Coyle, & Lyons, 2004, p. 403). Many theorists explored the ways in which masculine identity—whether gender self-identification, body image, or social in-group affiliation—is constructed and reconstructed through entertainment media.[4] Masculine stereotypes exist throughout western culture and have real effects on male gender identity[5] and on the relationship between violence and masculinity.[6] Some games use exaggerated male forms that exploit stereotypes of gendered bodies in pursuit of enticing character aesthetics.

Similarly, images of women in entertainment media, specifically those that cater to a male audience (the majority), highlight "the pervasive sexualization, objectification, and dehumanization of women in visual media" (Tylka & Calogero, 2011, p. 461). Media can, however, be used to educate and counteract dominant social structures.[7] The male gaze of mainstream media and society overall, though at times nuanced, and the objectification of women is well documented in feminist media theory.[8] The cultural and personal influences of these trends maintain patriarchal systems of dominance and undermine opportunities for men to develop in alternative ways without becoming vulnerable (Hargreaves & Tiggemann, 2009) or for them to be successful through alternate means.[9]

Masculinities are reinforced through entertainment media in many countries, not just the United States. Derné (2002) expressed valid points that exist across national borders, stating that "men are often attracted to transnational media depictions of male violence as the basis of male identity ... [and often handle anxieties] by rooting their own national identity in ... gender subordination that men regard as traditional" (p. 144). This may explain the desire on the part of game developers to cater to the supposed majority audience, young males, and the acceptance on the part of players of traditional (inequitable) power structures and aesthetic exaggerations of gendered bodies in interactive media characterizations. The vast majority of game developers function in a for-profit paradigm and therefore need to appeal to buying audiences. Gender is thus commoditized, and imagination is constrained by the demands of a market economy (increasingly unregulated capitalism).

Past research focused on the physiological and psychological influences of desensitization to violence through video games, film, and television with varying blame attributed to the potential desensitization and gendering of violent images presented for purposes of entertainment.[10] Mass media and academic sources attribute violent media with a power to influence real behaviors in its viewers. The high number of alternative variables that may in fact result in violent behavior and violent expressions of (traditionally masculine) identity make pinpointing causes nearly impossible.[11] Evidence is inconclusive as to the validity of aggression

Figure 5.1 Screenshot of *Dragon's Crown*. Dragon's Crown [Video game]. (2013). Osaka, Japan: Vanillaware.

tests in laboratory settings that link violent imagery with violent behavior.[12] Differences between study participants in terms of age, race, and sexuality must be considered before generalizations can be made based on these conceptions.

The media industry or *culture industry* has long held great influence over the general public with its elite ability to control access to the production and distribution of mass media.[13] This influences societies' exposure to art, music, information, and style. From the entertainment industry to the press, "the whole world is made to pass through the filter of the culture industry" (Horkheimer & Adorno, 2002, p. 2). This mass production of information and culture, controlled by a few powerful producers, directors, and corporations, subjects societies across the globe, especially in technologically advanced countries, to a ruthless uniformity of culture driven by capitalism and political interests.

The control of the culture industry shifted slightly in recent decades as technology became more accessible. Personal communication devices, instant Internet access, personal recording, and video technology at low prices allowed the individual to influence the culture industry in terms of accountability, trends, and the potential for social action. As bottom-up media continues to grow, will the culture industry continue to shape the identity of individuals in the general public, or will individuals reclaim and express their identities via new-found access to new media technology? Similarly, the ways in which the public responds to and learns from interactive media in entertainment is telling of the social influence of culture, the culture industry, and technology. Despite potential future shifts, the current entertainment industry is still the primary producer of (perhaps reflected) cultural trends.

Discourse regarding interactive media influences supports the continuation of this control despite opportunities for alternate voices through increased access to technology. With conformity as the norm, the social and gender-specific identities of consumers have largely been molded by their exposure to this mass-produced culture.[14] Traditional gender roles and familiar stories sell games, as evidenced by games like *Cooking Mama: Cook Off* (2007).

Though many interactive media products are extremely creative and unique, most rely on very similar stories and characters that are simply branded differently with new graphics; they do not fundamentally push cultural boundaries.[15] *Catherine* (2011) and *Portal* (2007) provide examples of games that stretch gender definitions by focusing on main characters that are insecure, or at least emotionally aware, men or strong, emotionally secure, women.

Wood (2011) discussed social learning theory and the important role of media[16] and described symbolic interactionism, stating that we learn who we are through communication with others specifically in terms of gender[17] as communicated through play activities with peers. Male

Figure 5.2 Common gender stereotypes. Super Mario Galaxy 2 [Video game]. (2010). Kyoto, Japan: Nintendo.

Figure 5.3 Screenshot of *Catherine*. Catherine [Video game]. (2011). Tokyo, Japan: Atlus.

stereotypes of aggression, confidence, and violence are often instances of contradiction. Wood (2011) described media representations[18] of men as lacking fuller character development and of women as passive sex objects, though there have been some mixing and complex characterization of both genders in more recent work. Through these hegemonic narratives, violence propagated and accepted by men, often against women, is normalized.[19]

Van Zoonen (1994) explained Althusser's concept that "people become subjects because of interpellation by ideology ... we are only able to make sense of ourselves and our social experiences within the limits and possibilities that language and the meaning system available in a given society set for us" (p. 24). Althusser used the term Ideological State Apparatuses (ISAs) for institutions such as religion, education, politics, and media.[20] The AAA interactive digital game industry falls directly into this categorization.

The level to which players identify with their characters, avatars, or in-game selves helps indicate the extent to which learning and internalization of ideological and identity markers might occur. The most prominent characteristics of interactive digital simulation narratives are those that align with traditional concepts of western cultural masculinity. Craig (1992) explored masculinities as problematic gender constructs informed by feminist thought.[21] The role of masculinities has been analyzed in terms of heavy metal music, comic books with super hero characters, beer commercials, television sitcoms, Hollywood war films, sports media, and violence and aggression in video games. Masculinity studies examine the ways images reinforce social constructs and stereotypical expectations of codes of gender performance.

Identity is culturally and psychologically tied to narrative, but it is critical that theorists base analyses not only on what people *do* or on outside conceptions of what has been *done*. Culturally sensitive research must also consider the *way* people do things "and what they say caused them to do what they did (Jerome Bruner, 1990, p. 16)" (Hammack, 2008, p. 222). Identity is defined as "ideology cognized through the individual engagement with discourse, made manifest in a personal narrative constructed and reconstructed across the life course, and scripted in and through social interaction and social practice" (Hammack, 2008, p. 222). This approach focuses on the interconnectedness of master narratives and personal narratives and aligns well with the idea of ergodic ontogeny—influences of society as well as specific interactive media artifacts on individual development. Identity is constructed, reconstructed, and changed through the real and the virtual, global and personal, the medium as well as the message.

Interactive digital games are not completely interactive at all times. They offer moments of interactivity but are also made up of non-interactive and only partially interactive play experiences. Drawing on a dystopian view of organic versus virtual bodies in cyberpunk literature, Newman[22] (2002) argued that many game studies are flawed and criticized previous studies that relied on "detached observation of players (often in 'laboratory conditions')" that examined "physiological change during active videogame play or the nature of post-videogame play behaviour, [while] more sensitive studies problematize the findings of previous investigations," noting the differences between reported and perceived experiences of interactivity (p. 408). Adequately complex critiques of identity and ideology construction through narratives in games are imperative. Storytelling can lead to *personal transformations*. "The right stories can open our hearts and change who we are. Digital narratives add another powerful element to this potential [for personal transformation] by offering us the opportunity to enact stories rather than to merely witness them" (Murray, 1998, p. 170). The new level of experiential narrative possible in interactive digital play is precisely what leads to personal transformation through ergodic ontogeny.

5.2 Immersion: Believability, Virtual Worlds, and the Uncanny Valley

Levels of immersion, connection, and player agency in digital gaming experiences are largely dependent on believability. The expectations that players bring to computer-mediated interactions help determine this believability, leading to either stronger or weaker identification with game systems, narratives, and characters. This is not meant to imply that simulations need to be entirely realistic or even have exceptionally well rendered graphics to impart meaning effectively to their audience. Experiences in virtual reality, or in the virtually immersive world of digital gaming, do not require appearances of reality to be believable and effective/affective.

Believability relies on a natural human tendency to disregard the unexpected, unless absolutely necessary, and reliance on common sense or general folk knowledge about the way the world works. If these criteria are kept in mind, then mediated virtual experiences may be equally believable without ever existing.[23] Pasquinelli's (2006, 2009) work supported the concept that though virtual objects and environments do not exist *in reality*, "virtual entities have an intersubjective character. It is possible, in fact, for multiple users, to make the same experience with a virtual scenario ... [so] experiences in VR are objective even if they do not include any real, existing entity" (2006, p. 201).

The mediated experiences of virtual interactive play do not rely on general expectations of everyday life, but on user/player expectations activated by the interactive digital or virtual experience that are "characterized as a judgment regarding the plausibility of a certain mediated experience, the judgment being positive when the experience respects the expectations of the subject which are activated by the contents and context of the experience itself" (Pasquinelli, 2006, p. 203).[24] Player expectations must coincide with the expectations that are activated by interaction with the game system. Though each player is somewhat different, certain responses are widely shared across media and acknowledged in terms of digital realism and believability.

The *uncanny valley* is a common example of predictable player, or simply *viewer*, response in which realism wanes as simulated human facial features near perfection. The concept of the uncanny valley effect began in the history of robotics.[25] "Roboticists have attempted to construct humanoid robots" to look identical to real humans; "Mori (1970) warned that robots should not be made too similar to real humans because such robots can fall into the 'uncanny valley,' where too high a degree of human realism evokes an unpleasant impression in the viewer" (Seyama & Nagayama, 2007, p. 337).[26] This assumption of player expectations is cited by many game designers, but the validity of the effect is unconfirmed[27] through psychological evidence. The aesthetic progression of the character Solid Snake, from the *Metal Gear* franchise between 1987 and 2014 (one of the few games with such longevity that also attempts a level of photorealism in character design), provides a chronological sample of changes in video game character models over the past decades.

The human visual system may process and define realism and abnormality separately, based on different visual features.[28] Video game characters may be accepted even when only slightly unrealistic, as long as features do not stray too far from human visual expectations of facial structures. An interesting consideration is the potential shift with increased realism of computer graphics. Will people born into an age of near photorealism have the same experiences of the uncanny valley as those who grew up before or during this technological advancement? As computer-mediated discourse, not only text- or code-based but also in terms of players' visual literacy, becomes more common place (increased new media and electracy), sensitivity to the uncanny valley may lessen, supporting the assumption that players/users understand mediation and

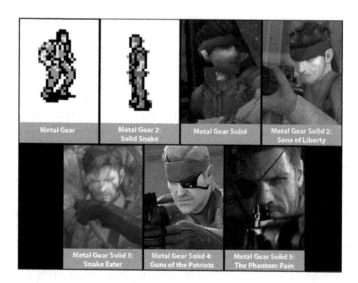

Figure 5.4 Metal Gear Solid character progression. Metal Gear [Video game]. (1987–2014). Tokyo, Japan: Konami.

experience virtual activities differently from activities in non-virtual environments. Players bring different expectations to game experiences because of their preconceptions of the medium.

The illusion of reality attempted by some simulated environments must also be analyzed in ethical terms. Players experience "multisensoriality and interactivity," which are credited with providing virtual reality systems/interfaces with "stronger means than traditional media (books, pictures, movies) for producing the illusion of reality" (Pasquinelli, 2009, p. 197). If players/users are misled, especially if there are ramifications of this deception in non-game realms, then interactivity and simulation become detrimental. Does the player experience the illusion of interactive digital gaming as *believability* (the convincing nature of a fictional experience) or as *deception* (such as a hoax/fraud, illusion of non-mediation, or the illusion of transportation/*being there* in a virtual world)?

Audiences do not believe fictional content or characters are *real* in the traditional sense.[29] Yet, the possibility of deception is present when the designer of an experience, whether another player in multiplayer or online interaction or the creator of the interactive model (game designer), has the "objective of inducing the user to misrepresent or misconstrue the origin of his experience" (Pasquinelli, 2009, p. 201). Risks include underestimating the real world effects of serious activities in the fictional world, being the prey of a hoax or fraud, or potentially underestimating the effects of one's own actions in the real world due to virtual experiences that are not physically possible (Pasquinelli, 2009, p. 209). These elements are some of the more obvious potential risks of social networks and online interactions, as well. Console games fall prey to similar concerns as online gaming via Xbox Live or the Play Station Network continues to gain popularity while fostering player expectations of strictly virtual repercussions.

5.3 Interview Data: Masculinities

Video games express, share, and reaffirm processes of gender self-identification through experiences of play that confirm or deny stereotypical biases. The interview data in this chapter provide insight into the influences of fantasy through play on later perceptions of reality as well as cultural identification and in/out group formation. Gender stereotypes are both supported (thematically) and contested (via sarcasm or conflicted expression) through this discourse regarding expectations of masculinity in United States culture. Virtual objectification[30] takes place when "the avatar is ... considered the embodiment of identity" (Dines & Humez, 2011, p. 574). Interview participants discussed their experiences growing up playing traditionally male-oriented games and connections forged with certain types of characters.

One participant explained that as a child, he did not feel his play habits were gender specific. However, he also stated that "when you look at it now and you give it a label ... there were lots of things that were more male-oriented, as opposed to 'gee, did you have tea parties', 'did you play *Barbie*', *Chutes and Ladders*, you know, Whatever! *My Little Pony*. None of that stuff." He continued, "it was mostly ... guy play. Even when I was playing with my sister it was mostly guy play because it was *Star Wars* and *G. I. Joe*." The overt catering to masculine tradition is clear within a few seconds of the opening of the *G.I. Joe* (1983–1986) children's television show.

A different participant discussed male-centered play in his youth and responded: "I feel like it was more about socialization. I was just around more of my male friends." He did not consider this trend a result of specific game content or social norms; it was just circumstance. Analysis of interview participants' discourse illuminated hegemonic expectations and assumptions and repeatedly evidenced participants' self-awareness of gendered stereotypes. The men who participated in this research expressed that they felt masculinity has some negative connotations and at the very least requires additional contextualization and discussion of its nuanced and complex iterations related to personal gender identity.

To understand how participants' self-reported identity markers fit into the larger cultural context of interactive digital play, it is necessary to establish foundational trends in general concepts of masculinity in the United States. Historically, cultural representations of masculinity "revolve around appearance (looks, clothes, strength), having male friends, heterosexuality (having a girlfriend, rejecting homosexuality), and getting respect primarily through economic status, athletics, toughness, and violence" (Phillips, 2005, p. 224). A clearer idea of how play influences

Figure 5.5 Screenshot of *G.I. Joe*. G.I. Joe: A Real American Hero [Television series]. (1985). Hasbro (Producer). Pawtucket, RI: Hasbro Studios.

real perceptions of self can be reached through an analysis of the ways men discuss their personal understandings of these cultural influences.

Participants expressed conscious awareness of gendered discourses and stereotypes that exist in United States society. Details of their speech patterns implicitly, and likely inadvertently, reaffirm some of these discourses. For example, they both directly stated and implied a connection between violence and masculinity. "'Naturalistic' gender discourses are reflected in discourses of war and violence and intimately link violence and hegemonic masculinity," which secures gendered divisions of violence and supports assumptions about male identity (Hatchell, 2006, p. 383). The relationship between violence and masculinity often goes unstated in casual conversation due to this naturalization.

Morality in game ethics was another topic that interview participants expressed in semi-contested ways; they related moral choices to a sense of personal superiority and downplayed the importance of friendship in their play experiences. The following pragmatic analyses explore the developmental aspects of cultural understanding, identity formation, and meaning-making in play activities.[31] Analysis of masculine discourse provides insight into the influences of fantasy in digital play on perceptions of the self in reality in terms of gender and other identity markers. Participants described their play activities, as youth and adults, as thematically violent. However, participants did not consider this to be their primary interest or reason for partaking in such activities. Violent games are established forms of acceptable male play in Western culture that foster traditional senses of superiority and power and provide convenient and socially non-threatening outlets for male bonding.[32] Friendship ties often evolve around the guise of overt or exaggerated masculinity. As Copper (C) explained when describing his current (adult) play and entertainment habits:

1. C: We play on the PlayStation network
2. C: which, as you <u>know</u>, is notoriously foul-mouthed
3. C: And at this point (.) the only reason we stay on
4. C: the PlayStation network is to let people know
5. C: that they shouldn't do that (1)
6. C: So if any one uses a::ny racial slurs <u>what</u>soever
7. C: we actually spend the next round ru::ining their <u>kill</u>-ratio.
8. C: And, um, and you know, just just ... (1)
9. C: talking about what's going on with us (.)
10. C: I mean, one guy lives in Japan now (.) he's stationed there.
11. C: Another guy's, you know, Texas and all that stuff (1)
12. C: So, usually it's about Sunday morning
13. C: when we can get together.
14. C: <u>Um</u> (1) and just (1) I think we play
15. C: maybe o::ne or two rounds (3)
16. C: Mostly we're just <u>chatting</u> (laughs)

Copper is very comfortable situating the goals for his own play with friends as morally superior to other online users, situating himself and those he is close to in a position of authority. This is an altruistic pursuit,[33] and online gaming is very often a breeding ground for hate speech and outward verbal abuse and bigotry (Hargrave & Livingstone, 2009). The lexical choice of phrases with slightly heightened intonation and vocabulary such as "notoriously foul-mouthed" (line 2), "racial slurs whatsoever" (line 6), or "kill ratio" (line 7) give this discourse a sense of authority and formality.

The second part of his statement, however, describes that despite playing a violent game, they do so more for the social aspect of play. This discourse is full of pauses and terms such as "and" (line 8), "um" (lines 8 and 14), and "you know" (lines 8 and 11) that break the flow of the speech act. Copper distances himself through ambiguity with his use of words and phrases such as the filler "and all that stuff" (line 11), hedging statements such as "so usually" (line 12), "about" (line 12), "maybe" (line 15), and "mostly" (line 16), or by repeating the word "just" sometimes in immediate succession (twice in line 8, lines 14 and 16) to normalize his discourse by implying that they are just (read as *simply*) "chatting" (line 16). The differences between the first and second half of this discourse suggest that he is less comfortable discussing interpersonal relationships, a commonly feminized topic.

In all cases, participants denied any direct connection between playing games with violent themes and experiences of real-life violence. However, a number of linguistic devices ultimately connected these two activities. The initial disavowal of any relation between play and reality may be due to participants' sensitivity to current popular media representations that often blame violent entertainment for the actions of violent people. "Because complex actions like violent behavior are multi-determined and develop over time, it is difficult to find direct cause-effect relationships between games and violence" (Power, 2009, p. 91). All participants stressed a clear distinction between enjoying violent themes in entertainment practices and acting outside the law in a violent way. For instance, George (G), a retired state trooper in his early 30's, stated:

1. G: I (.) I'd like to be the person who keeps trying to say
2. G: and keeps trying to convince himself
3. G: that he was not a big first person shooter gamer
4. G: but the reality is (1) I remember when Halo came out (.)
5. G: and that was hu::ge (1)
6. G: It's got some story, but it's rife with violence (1.5) …
7. G: I think it's actually a lot easier to get a game where
8. G: you're going to go shoot this or shoot that.
9. G: But at the same time (.) ye::ah, it was hard
10. G: n::ot to (1) enjoy it.

Figure 5.6 Screenshot of *Halo 4*. Halo 4 [Video game]. (2012). Redmond, WA: Microsoft Studios.

George wanted to avoid masculine stereotypes related to enjoyment of violent games but admits to enjoying play activities that have violent themes. George would "like to be" (line 1) a person that keeps "trying to say" (line 1) things that "convince himself" (line 2) of the contrary. However, such assertions make it clear from the beginning of his statement that the perlocutionary[34] effect of this discourse overall is to admit that those disavowals are not actually the case, that he is fully aware of this false disavowal, and that his listener should be as well. He pauses before admitting at the end, without sarcasm or other distancing devices, that he does in fact "… enjoy it" (line 10). *Halo* (2001) provides quick action with the objective of killing as many aliens (importantly non-human forms) as efficiently as possible.

Assertions of desired distancing from stereotypical enjoyment of violence continued through statements suggesting that those types of entertainment do not always provide enjoyable experiences but often serve more as confirmations of male normativity and status. When discussing his recent experiences of entertainment, in this instance changing the topic to film with overtly violent themes, Copper (C) stated:

1. C: I mean, uh, to be fair, like, uh I (1)
2. C: in my group of friends
3. C: we do have kind of an iron man kind of method
4. C: for watching movies.
5. C: You know, we're like, okay (.) can you handle
6. C: this whole film?
7. C: (gruff voice) Can you <u>do</u> it, <u>bro</u>?!
8. C: (normal voice) You know, so, watching Human Centipede
9. C: or really <u>really</u> brutal movies, and it's (2)
10. C: I don't actually find it enjo::yable?

11. C: But like (.) can I get through this
12. C: Um (.) honestly (.) uh. I think that a lot times (.)
13. C: the (.) the flatter and more realistic the violence is
14. C: the more it bothers me (.)
15. C: Like I can't watch torture scenes, no matter what.
16. C: If I have the ability, I will fast-forward.

Phrases like "to be fair" (line 1) and "honestly" (line 12) during hesitations ("um" and "uh," uttered a total of four times with numerous pauses (.) and the word "like" uttered four times as well) imply that Copper is providing insight that might not generally be made available to others and perhaps that he is making concessions to the overall identity he is comfortable publicly portraying. The use of an altered deep or gruff voice and words like "bro" (line 7), "iron man" (line 3), and "brutal" (line 9) are displays of exaggerated reference to masculine stereotypes. *Prosody*, the intonation and rhythm of speech, is "an interactional resource for contextualizing the valence of [information] ...-sequentially organized activities strongly associated with emotional displays of joy and sorrow" (Beach, 2000, p. 381). Copper's use of an intentionally deeper voice is almost mocking expectations of masculinity, and his admission at the end of an aversion to "flatter" or "more realistic" violence (line 13) supports this disjuncture between his real opinions and those he thinks are expected of his gender.

5.4 Ergodic Ontogeny: Demonstrated in Discourse

One of the primary themes that emerged from the sociolinguistic exploration of interactive play experience was a balking at hegemony. Ergodic ontogeny, including development of personal gender representation, is informed by childhood and adult play activities and expressed through discourses of interactive play. The ways in which participants expressed their interest or disinterest in certain ideas, actions, or identities provided insight into the factors that influence identity construction. Participants referenced similar childhood play activities, most likely due to their closeness in age and exposure to similar popular cultural influences.[35] Many recalled occasionally playing in mixed-gendered groups, yet most of their preferred play activities centered on characters and themes that were culturally marketed to an exclusively young male audience, such as *G.I. Joe*, *Star Wars*, and *Mega Man*, which resulted in more male friends than female, especially before high school. Female friends were said to be welcome to join in play, but the themes and game content were so traditionally male-centric that they were often excluded or chose not to participate.

In keeping with hegemonic structures, analyses of military male discourse support a construction of masculinity "that is symbolically dominant over others" in which "men position themselves as more morally oriented, self-disciplined, physically capable, emotionally controlled, martially skilled, or intelligent" (Hinojosa, 2010, p. 179). Yet, interview participants tended to distance themselves from overt statements that supported the superiority of men in society. This may be due to cultural sensitivity to the issue and also possibly to the fact that they were being interviewed by a female researcher. For example, one research participant who served in the U.S. Army, Leon (L), remarked:

1. L: I had specific <u>levels</u> that I enjoyed?
2. L: more than others (.) and would specifically play for those
3. L: and I wouldn't care about progressing the sto::ry.

Leon asserted that competitive, social, rule-based, or narrative-driven incentives never connected with him in video game play. The stress of the words "levels" (line 1) and "story" (line 3) clarify the distinction between these two play elements for Leon. *Levels* have activities within them without necessarily being narratively goal-driven, and players can, as one participant put it, "just destroy everything," whereas a story or narrative (commonly feminized topics) implies a deeper level of interest or meaning that is outside the realm of traditional masculine acceptability.

Leon's discourse is reminiscent of common speech acts that position men, especially as boys, as interested only in conflict and physicality, rather than more feminized concepts like stories (recall his drawn out use of the word "sto::ry" in line 3) that might imply caring about characters or becoming emotionally involved in play. Stereotypical masculine discourses of domination and destruction are evident in Leon's statement, as well. His remarks began with the phrase "well, I just ..." (line 1) implying that the discourse is justified and perhaps logical. His speech in the excerpt above is direct with few hesitations or fillers, other than a brief pause (line 2). This implies clarity of thought and expression and a confidence in his beliefs and the ways in which such statements will be interpreted.

Similarly, he stated a direct relationship between virtual experiences in games and experiences during his time in the military, but did re-frame the idea of violence. Leon's response:

1. L: Well, there's definitely a correlation (2)
2. L: I don't know about vi::olence, but (1)
3. L: more action.
4. L: But <u>violent</u> action. (2)
5. L: Violence is (.) yeah (.) I would say.

This discourse is far less direct, using syntactic modifiers to qualify his statements, and far more segmented with distinct pauses after every few words. The drawn out word "violence" (line 4) implies that perhaps that is too strong of a term for what he is trying to express. This is a face-saving attempt to avoid making a direct connection between enjoying violent games and performing violent actions. Leon participated in an interview process with an expectation of honesty and seems to have felt compelled to say "well. ..." (line 1) yes, there is a connection, but then repeatedly used hedging statements to immediately distance himself from that assertion, such as "I don't know" (line 3), "but ..." (line 4), and the final lack of conclusion in the confused statement "yeah, I would say" (line 5).

Interview participants felt compelled to reject *normative discourses*. Normative masculine discourses of violence are evidenced repeatedly in terms of acceptable language use, activity, and displays of emotion. Masculine discourses displayed through the interviews discussed in this book support traditional cultural values of masculinity in terms of domination, destruction, and strength that are reproduced, at least partially, in conjunction with the influence of video game play activities. Verbal expressions of superiority and anger, in conversational contexts, were comfortable topics for these speakers. Emotion, narrative, and interpersonal relationships were less comfortable subjects of discussion. Participants demonstrated complex processes of identity construction as evidenced by nuanced switches between discussions of play experiences and reality.

Male hegemony was affirmed but also positioned as a framework to be mocked or disavowed by modern or progressive members of society. All of the participants distanced themselves to an extent from stereotypes of overt masculine identity but to some extent continued to behave and speak according to them. This demonstrates participants' familiarity with engrained gendered roles in society and their conscious awareness of the potential influence of video game play on self-identity construction during developmental years. The choice to abide by or challenge rules and expectations for play activities, and the inclusion of other players or teammates, influences how players see themselves and others in and out of the game world. Many interactive digital games are shifting away from conceptions of player agency that are bound to set and limited rules-based environments, thus becoming more open.[36] Agency will have more to do with freedom to explore the potential of a virtual experience in unexpected ways as games evolve. Future research should explore the ways in which these changes in play influence the internalization of game experiences for children growing up while playing interactive video games from more recent decades.

An obvious omission in the current interview data is the female gamer and the relation of play practices of girls to gender identity and ideology construction. This preliminary study focused solely on male discourse as a function of traditional stereotypes[37] and cultural expectations of masculinity in order to determine emergent themes of ergodic ontogeny. Female discourses of play activities will provide insight into this process as well. Many researchers focus on alternate populations of gamers, a trend that must continue.[38] Future analyses of linguistic expressions of ergodic ontogeny should include more detailed contextual structures such as generational, cultural, and geographic differences among the populations interviewed. Intentionally limited and specific in its focus, this case study provided a starting point for thematic trends through insight into the ways in which players internalize social expectations of identity through video game play, construct personal ideologies based on game narrative, self-identify in relation to virtual characters, and reaffirm cultural ideologies.

5.5 Self-Identification and New Media Identity Construction

The ubiquity of new media technologies changes how media operate within societies and the influence they have on individuals. Hayles (1999) provided a starting point for exploring identity in terms of new media and the post-human;[39] she advocated that the "overlay" between the *enacted* body and the *represented* body is not a "natural inevitability but a contingent production, mediated by a technology that has become so entwined with the production of identity that it can no longer meaningfully be separated from the human subject" (p. xiii). This complication of the individual (human) body and its agency is linked to the concept of cyborgs (human-machine hybrids) and a blurring of the self and the computerized other, if it is an *other* at all.

Even decades after her writing, individuals still report a clear sense of self in reality, unmarred by virtual representation. This may simply be a way to cling to historical representations and understandings of the human[40] while avoiding outward acknowledgment of the depth of modern connections to virtual selves. People have forgotten, or may never have known, what it felt like to *not* be inherently tied to, informed by, identified through technology, and therefore do not know the difference. This way of experiencing the world, the blurring of the virtual and the real, can be directly applied to understanding ergodic ontogeny through interactive digital game experiences. Though Hayles argued for an implicit and unavoidable melding, a loss of the human outside this realm, my interview participants reported both connection and disjuncture with the real and the virtual.[41]

The concept of *enaction* is "the active engagement of an organism with the environment as the cornerstone of the organism's development" (Hayles, 1999, p. 155). This focus on action within an environment is the very development described by ergodic ontogeny. Hayles specifically differentiated this *embodiment* from the concept of the body itself in that it is always relative "to some set of criteria ... In contrast to the body, embodiment is contextual, enmeshed within the specifics of place, time, physiology, and culture, which together compose enactment"

(p. 196). Ultimately, Hayles' analysis is applied to concepts of cyber theory, humanity, and philosophy rather than the directed analysis of this book, which addresses the way we play and experience specific interactive digital games. Hayles (1999) posited that "the distributed cognition of the emergent human subject correlates with ... becomes a metaphor for – the distributed cognitive system as a whole, in which 'thinking' is done by both human and nonhuman actors" (p. 290). Positioning research within the post-human context has very specific implications about what can be known and how meaning-making takes place.

Whether identity is entirely enmeshed in cybernetic culture remains in contention, as does the extent to which the connection between human and machine[42] effects identity creation. Virtual realities in game worlds can only be as real as the experiences of their players. Hayles (1999) rejected the original feedback loop perspective, and stated that there is no world "'out there' that exists apart from us ... only what our systemic organization allows us to see" (p. 11) and that virtuality is "the cultural perception that material objects are interpenetrated by information patterns"; the perception of "virtuality facilitates the development of virtual technologies, and the technologies reinforce the perception" (p. 13–14).[43] The role of the user (player) and the complexity of computer systems distinguish electronic media from other communicative forms, which in turn shapes the way modern human epistemology functions in the world.

Literary texts are shapers of technological meaning and cultural context. Through electronic media, however, players absorb information with no one-to-one correspondence between signifier and signified.[44] This reflects the mediation through the screen in which the viewer's "consciousness moves through the screen to become the POV [point-of-view], leaving behind the body as an unoccupied shell" (Hayles, 1999, p. 38) at which moment the point-of-view is abstracted, losing any spatial components. The interactive space is "narrativized by the POV's movement through it" (Hayles, 1999, p. 39).[45]

The nature of digital environments is a crucial component of ergodic ontogeny. Murray (1998) outlined four properties of digital environments, including procedural (executing a series of rules, feedback loops), participatory (in which the interactor can induce certain behavior or responses), spatial (representing navigable space, not describing it through word or image as in books/film), and encyclopedic (which can store and retrieve vast quantities of information). "The experience of being transported to an elaborately simulated place is pleasurable in itself, regardless of the fantasy content" (Murray, 1998, p. 98). However, Murray (1998) warned that this "liminal trance is so inherently fragile" that narrative art forms must find ways of sustaining it, especially because good stories serve an important function for adults, "something safely outside ourselves (because it is made up by someone else) upon which we can project our feelings" inhabiting a "magical borderland" (p. 100). Participation on the part of the (w)reader/user/player makes this *borderland* all the more subjective, delicate, and potentially evocative. The interactor is not an *author* for Murray, but is an *agent*.

Murray (1998) argued that "enacted events have a transformative power that exceeds both narrated and conventionally dramatized events because we assimilate them as personal experiences" (p. 170). When pondering how digital environments might deliver the level of engagement and plot of past media, she suggested designers must "allow them to write procedurally; to anticipate all the twists of the kaleidoscope, all the actions of the interactor; and to specify not just the events of the plot but also the rules by which those events would occur" (1998, p. 185).[46] Games with multilayered potentials for ergodic ontogeny, as described in Chapter 4 (*Fable*, *Knights of the Old Republic*, the *Mass Effect* series, etc.), have in many ways reached Murray's utopian conception of a cyber drama, but without anticipating every turn, rather allowing for flexibility and change dependent on the player.

The player is a true agent in interactive digital media play, enacting embedded ideologies through virtual experiences. There are many varied explorations of the ways in which interactivity in digital games influences identity and ideology. The teaching qualities of game experiences are particularly poignant in terms of the ways players learn ideological concepts and take away a sense of identification with certain characters from game play into the real world: ergodic ontogeny. Gee (2008) stated explicitly that through interactive digital play, "players learn to view the virtual world through the eyes and values of a distinctive identity (e.g., Solid Snake in *Metal Gear Solid*) or one they themselves have built from the ground up (e.g., in *The Elder Scrolls III: Morrowind*)" (p. 1028).[47] Good video games are those that allow the player to produce as well as consume the narrative and play experience (Gee, 2008). This relates to the connections established between user and computer, human and machine. For example, an open-ended game like *The Elder Scrolls* series is, in the end, a different game for each player. Gee (2008) argued that players in fact co-design the game in this regard through implementation of individual and personalized choices and actions during play.

This increased level of personal involvement in the medium itself returns analysis to game pioneer Nolan Bushnell's law[48] of why players play, why they feel compelled to continue playing. "Good games stay within, but at the outer edge of, the player's 'regime of competence' … they feel 'doable,' but challenging. This makes them pleasantly frustrating – a flow state for human beings" (Gee, 2008, p. 1029). Gee (2008) provided an example of a war-simulator game and explained that the game teaches players to think, value, and act like a soldier but that the in-game, virtual characters "control different parts of the domain" of knowledge and that "we get the whole domain only when we put their knowledge together.

Figure 5.7 Ideologies. Metal Gear Solid 4: Guns of the Patriots [Video game]. (2008). Tokyo, Japan: Konami.

The knowledge is distributed between them. A human (the player) shares knowledge with a virtual reality (the soldiers)" (p. 1035).

In digital realms, the player is fully immersed in the actions, values, and perspectives of the character. Ideology is an essential component of learning. "Adopting a certain set of values and a particular worldview is intimately connected to doing the activities and having the experiences that constitute any specific domain of knowledge" (Gee, 2008, p. 1036). This is, again, why interactive agentive digital play is particularly evocative in terms of ontogeny. Developing a sense of self informed by experiences both within and outside of virtual experience is impossible to avoid.

5.6 Role of the Player

Immersion in interactivity, embodiment, and enaction in virtual play may be unique to each individual. Ideas of post-humanism, interactivity, and ideology are meaningless without the individual through which these concepts are expressed. Sutton-Smith (2001) described the basis of play as situated in the psychology of individual players with a focus on freedom of form, value, experience, language, and consciousness of playfulness.[49] Definitions of play in terms of the self are dependent on the self being discussed and must include consideration of the cultural, social, class-based, and gender differences that may be present. The player brings certain expectations to game experiences and is also shaped by experiences of agentive action.

The role of the player is tied to interactivity and personal agency. Tanenbaum and Tanenbaum (2010) offered a means of exploring player agency through *speech act* theory.[50] This method is employed in order to investigate feelings of agency in interactive gaming experiences in terms of communicative competence of both game player and game designer in digital realms with increasingly high levels of so-called freedom. They alter the traditional definition of agency from *choice* or *freedom* to *commitment to meaning*. It is crucial, therefore, to remember the expectation that player choice and freedom will change the anticipated progression of gameplay, and "'interactors can only act within the possibilities that have been established by the writing and programming' (Murray 1997)" (Tanenbaum & Tanenbaum, 2010, p. 12). Players are not simply interacting with a system, but performing an improvised story. "Designers and performers are in a type of conversation with each other, mediated by the game, and their ability to commit to meanings and follow through on those commitments are crucial" (Tanenbaum & Tanenbaum, 2010, p. 14).

Players activate and deactivate expectations and desires that can be satisfied within game experiences.[51] Ultimately, as the previous chapters detailed, academic and scientific explorations of video game influence need not be categorized as *either* players interacting within a system *or* performers enacting a story, but as a combination of *both*. *Half-Life 2* (2004), for example, effectively guides the player while providing a sense of player agency: the player commits to meaning and actions within the game at each moment. The player is in control of his/her character at all times and prompted to perform actions (picking up a can, for example, which while narratively logical also teaches the player how to interact with the game world via the controller). Various cues guide the action; NPCs push or block retreat, dialogue interactions take place in the direction needed for the game to progress, and available pathways are limited. The result is that players follow the direction that the game designers desire. Yet, by allowing the player to navigate these playable moments, the sense of agency is maintained.

Figure 5.8 Screenshot of *Half-Life 2*. Half-Life 2 [Video game]. (2004). Bellevue, WA: Valve Corporation.

Ergodic ontogeny, as influenced by these agentive elements of game play, is only effectively understood after applying interdisciplinary, multi-lensed critical analyses to the key elements of interactive digital play—a daunting, but not impossible, task if researchers are willing to cross disciplinary lines and value both qualitative and quantitative research in science (computer, information systems, biology, psychology) and humanities (media, communication, literature, visual art, ludology, culture) to explore real-world influences on virtual/synthetic worlds, and vice versa. Researchers must value the historically situated relationship between interactive environments/activities and real-world experiences, especially as related to highly contested and emotionally evocative topics, from a critical perspective that embraces connections between the virtual and the real while maintaining an acute awareness of the lack of explicit ties between *playing* at actions and actually *acting*. If simulations or synthetic worlds experienced through computer-mediated action are the future directions of leisure activity, learning, and potentially commerce, politics, or other forms of social post-human interaction,[52] then a critical understanding of these technologies is all the more essential. Separations of work and leisure are less clear, and the blurring of this boundary is likely to continue and increase.[53] New media will continue to converge and eventually blend into all aspects of everyday/ real life. The process of ergodic ontogeny will be increasingly critical in understanding how cultures reproduce, share, and create knowledge on the individual level.

Notes

1 Van Dijk (2006) approached ideological analysis through language, but his descriptions are not without limitations. He provided a definition of ideology as a system of ideas within the frameworks of discourse, cognition, and society. Belief systems are the ideas of belief themselves, not the practices or social structures based on them. Ideologies are socially shared by group members but are not needed or developed by all collectivities of social actors, only certain groups that share beliefs about their fundamental conditions and ways of existence and reproduction. These fundamental, core, or axiomatic ideas serve to organize, control, and provide coherence (cognitive function) to socially shared knowledge or attitudes (Van Dijk, 2006). Ideologies are gradually acquired, changed, and lost. Group ideology is usually stable with variability existing primarily on individual levels through multiple experiences and discourses over a long period of time. Van Dijk's elaborate definition implies an objective perspective that fails to account for how certain ideologies acquire dominance while others do not.

2 The most useful contribution of Van Dijk's (2006) article in the present context is the system of breaking down language use in terms of in-group and out-group self-identification. Ideologies are acquired and reproduced by discourse through strategies such as positive self-presentation and negative other-presentation, discursive ways to enhance or mitigate concepts of our/their and good/bad. This is highly contextual, however, and can be

found at all levels of communication including meaning, form, and action. Therefore, it becomes difficult to understand if this definition of ideology is truly helpful in determining how any ideology can ever become *knowledge* for a community or group and whether or not that knowledge is in any way stable or complete. The limitations of ideological discourse analysis include intentionality, ideological (over)interpretation, contextualization, power/presupposition, and critical analysis (Van Dijk, 2006). Yet, Van Dijk seems to take for granted the power structures that lead to, reinforce, and make change difficult in these ideologies. He does not discuss the enactment or performance of power, a key element that must be added to any analysis of ideological discourse. All knowledge is ideological and never absolute.

3 The use of *us/we* versus *them* is a common indicator of in/out group identification in linguistic terms.

4 See Hobza and Rochlen (2009), Morrison and Halton (2009), Parasecoli (2005), Soulliere and Blair (2006), and Weber (2006).

5 Reproduced social norms affect female members of society, as well, of course. Acceptable expressions of emotions like anger for men imply the inappropriate nature of similar expressions for women in complex ways. Recall Brown's *Raising Their Voices* (1998) as mentioned in Chapter 4. Expressions of emotions manifest differently depending on social norms for both genders; differences are often influenced by class, culture, and race.

6 See Bordo (1999), Farquhar and Wasylkiw (2007), Hobza, Walker, Yakushko, and Peugh (2007), and Kimmel (1996, 2008).

7 See Keller and Brown (2002) and Tylka and Calogero (2011).

8 For further reading, see Dines and Humez (2011), Stewart, Cooper, Stewart, and Friedley (2003), Van Zoonen (1994), and Wood (2011).

9 See Butler (1990, 1993) and Johnson, McCreary, and Mills (2007).

10 See Carnagey, Anderson, and Bushman (2007), Cassell and Jenkins (1998), Cline, Croft, and Courrier (1973), Funk, Baldacci, Pasold, and Baumgardner (2004), and Klinger, Hamilton, and Cantrell (2001).

11 See Birkland and Lawrence (2009), Burns and Crawford (1999), and Feshbach and Singer (1971).

12 See Ferguson, Smith, Miller-Stratton, Fritz, and Heinrich (2008).

13 The phrase *culture industry* was coined by Horkheimer and Adorno (2002) to imply the overarching sociocultural impact of entertainment media.

14 As technology changes, knowledge of the ways people come together to make meaning through collective intelligence is critical to our understanding of identity and culture. This applies not only to the effects of media change, but to the affects as well. Clough and Halley (2007) argued, "the perspective of the affects requires us constantly to pose as a problem the relation between actions and passions, between reason and the emotions... an ontology of the human that is constantly open and renewed" (p. x). This parallels the concepts put forth by Rice and O'Gorman (2008) supporting an approach to cultural understanding that takes into account experiences of the individual. "Affect refers generally to bodily capacities to affect and be affected or the augmentation or diminution of a body's capacity to act, to engage, and to connect, such that auto affection is linked to the self-feeling of being alive" (Clough & Halley, 2007, p. 2). The *affective turn* marks "an intensification of self-reflexivity (processes turning back on themselves to act on themselves) in information/communication systems, including the human body; in archiving machines, including all forms of media technologies and human memory" (Rice & O'Gorman, 2008, p. 3). This self-reflexive loop of

the real, the imaginary, and the symbolic is essential to an understanding of the relationship between new media technology and personal identity.

15 Some exceptions to this rule are discussed in Chapter 2.

16 Wood (2011) explained Carol Gilligan's approach to morality and relationships in terms of comprehensive cultural theories.

17 Gender roles can be understood through standpoint theory, which states that social interactionism exists within socially constructed groups. This is important in terms of Hegelian power relationships: if power relationships exist in society, then there can be no single (objective, independent) view of social life (Wood, 2011, p. 58–59).

18 Wood (2011) focused on advertising: the repeated visuals that people think they are immune to that teach social expectations for interaction, specifically in terms of women as dependent, incompetent, caregivers, victims, and sex objects. Such advertisements and media narratives motivate us to consume (products or media texts) by playing on insecurities. Both men and women, therefore, assess themselves unfairly in terms of social knowledge learned through the repetition of such trends.

19 There are a number of varied approaches to understanding media influence on gender identity construction. *Communication and Gender* (Stewart et al., 2003) is a source for discussion of the primary theories researchers use to discuss the ways in which gender is communicated through media. Stewart et al. (2003) explained social learning theory that explores representations of same-sex models at home and in media (p. 18), cognitive development theory, a la Piaget, which supports the idea that children switch at some point from receiving gender information to seeking it (p. 21), social role theories (p. 23), Gilligan's moral voice theory (p. 24–25), and symbolic interaction that asserts gender is learned from significant others (p. 24). It is important to remember Kimmel's (1996, 2008) point, as well, that both genders are equally socially constructed.

20 Van Zoonen (1994) also discussed Gramsci's description of hegemony as that which refers to the process "by which general consent is actively sought for the interpretations of the ruling class. Dominant ideology becomes invisible because it is translated into 'common sense', appearing as the natural unpolitical state of things accepted by each and everyone" (p. 24). Semiology, analysis of visual and verbal signs, examines connotative codes: "implied or associative meanings of signs" as opposed to their literal meaning (Van Zoonen, 1994, p. 25). This informs the pragmatic analysis provided for the interview data included in the following sections of this chapter.

21 This conception was furthered in the works of Bordo (1999), Cassel and Jenkins (1998), Kimmel (1996, 2008), and others.

22 Newman (2002) did not support stereotypes of masculinity or claims of game sexism. Rather, "the embodied, experiential model of player–character relationships that contests the significance of representation within the feedback loop of interactive engagement is offered as a means of gaining a better and more sensitive understanding of this important new medium" so that players might avoid oppressive representations of self (p. 406).

23 Recall the example of visual representations of one's heartbeat altering self-perception mentioned in Chapter 1.

24 Pasquinelli (2006) explained that suspension of disbelief, "deactivation of certain expectations," may involve the "perceptual and motor-perceptual or interactive conditions that are associated with the narrative elements of a story" (p. 203). If certain expectations of realism in a virtual environment are deactivated, then the player will experience this reality as believable.

25 Kang's *Sublime Dreams of Living Machines* (2011) explored conceptions of the human in relation to machines, specifically in terms of automata. By tracing the cultural development of current understandings of automata, as well as the historical time periods from which such definitions are drawn, he illustrated connections between what it means to be human and humanity's reflection in living and non-living entities and creations, a topic that certainly has implications for virtual characters.

26 More recently, "Mori's hypothesis has been adopted as a guideline for designing the physical appearance of robots" and, more importantly in terms of simulations and gaming, the appearance of "agents in virtual reality" (Seyama & Nagayama, 2007, p. 338).

27 This is why Seyama and Nagayama decided to conduct a study to measure viewer responses depending on the degree of realism of images shown.

28 Seyama and Nagayama (2007) demonstrated that the uncanny valley "emerged only when the face images involved abnormal features. Thus, to fully understand the nature of the uncanny valley, we need to consider the effects of both the realism and the abnormality of artificial human appearance" (p. 348).

29 Pasquinelli (2009) explained that audiences, readers, and players "do not hold existence beliefs about fictional contents...responses to fictional contents are similar but never identical to responses to corresponding nonfictional contents (no one calls the police in response to what one sees on horror movies or in violent video games)" (p. 200).

30 For example, Dines and Humez (2011) referenced Alan Klein's *Little Big Men* (1993) in which he stated that "muscles...are about more than just the functional ability of men to defend home and hearth or to perform heavy labor" (p. 267). Muscles, in fact, define ideals of the male form despite drastic variation in physical traits of individuals.

31 See Bateson (1955), Furth (1967), Piaget (1962), Sutton-Smith (1966), and Wertsch (1984).

32 See Bordo (1999), Farquhar and Wasylkiw (2007), Hobza et al. (2007), and Kimmel (1996, 2008).

33 Specific characteristics of the research population must be kept in mind. This speaker may feel superior due to a position of authority professionally, due to an age discrepancy between himself and other (likely younger) online players, or a myriad of other potential factors.

34 Perlocutionary acts are speech acts with consequence, how the discourse is intended to persuade or otherwise influence.

35 See Cassell and Jenkins (1998) and Kimmel (1996, 2008).

36 It is important to distinguish between open world games, in which the player may move freely in any direction with realistically loading environments, and sandbox games, in which players may interact with almost all assets in the game world, provoking emergent play that takes new forms and unexpected directions.

37 Different expressions of identity were explored in terms of a "fluidity of masculinities [that] recreates power relationships between males, power [then] reinvents itself in discourses of hegemonic masculinity through its vested interest in violence" (Hatchell, 2006, p. 388).

38 See Beavis and Charles (2007), Jenson and de Castell (2010), and Schott and Horrell (2000).

39 Hayles' (1999) view of the post-human "privileges informational pattern over material instantiation, so that embodiment in a biological substrate is seen as an accident of history rather than an inevitability of life" such that

the body is simply a prosthesis with "no essential differences or absolute demarcations between bodily existence and computer simulation" (p. 2–3).

40 Recall Chapter 3 in which Levi professed a disconnection between enjoyment of violence in play versus reality and Chapter 5 in which George would "like to" deny a connection between real and virtual experience.

41 Hayles (1999) used the term *autopoiesis* (self-making), equated with human experience, to build on the work of Maturana. Humberto Maturana, working with Francisco Varela, spearheaded what Hayles refered to as the "second wave of cybernetics, from 1960 to 1985," moving in a new direction that acknowledged the observer (p. 131). This conception values the observer not as one who discerns "preexisting systems," but as one who creates them "through the very act of observation" (Hayles, 1999, p. 131).

42 Machine rather than human- and electronically-mediated narrative or ludic elements of a game/text.

43 Hayles (1999) explained that Shannon's information theory defines information as a "probability function with no dimensions, no materiality, and no necessary connection with meaning...only when the message is encoded in a signal for transmission through a medium...does it assume material form"; before that, "no message is ever sent" (p. 18). Claude Shannon's paper "A Mathematical Theory of Communication" (1948) founded information theory, which later expanded from purely mathematical and computational purposes and was applied to semantic communication forms (Shannon & Weaver, 1963).

44 Hayles (1999) carried the "instabilities implicit in Lacanian floating signifiers one step further," stating that information technologies create "flickering signifiers, characterized by their tendency toward unexpected metamorphoses, attenuations, and dispersions" (p. 30), and discussed literary texts as more than "passive conduits" (p. 21).

45 The narrator "becomes not so much a scribe as a cyborg authorized to access the relevant codes" (Hayles, 1999, p. 44); "when narrative functionalities change, a new kind of reader is produced by the text" (Hayles, 1999, p. 47).

46 At the time of her writing, Murray (1998) suggested that "the story line in most gaming software can be described in terms of [only] two or three morphemes (fight bad guy, solve puzzle, die)," a simplicity that has been challenged in recent years by programmers with additional resources as well as an eye to expanding the definition of the word *game* (p. 197).

47 Gee (2008) described a trend that "over the last few years, interest in the contrast between popular culture and school has risen," and that modern youth seem to "engage in deeper learning in their popular culture than they do in school, especially schools devoted to skill-and-drill in the service of passing standardized tests" (p. 1028).

48 Recall the discussion of Bushnell's Law in Chapter 2. Games should be easy to learn, yet difficult to master.

49 Though many of these aspects are dictated to a certain extent by a video game's code, Gadamer's definition of play may still be applied given the inclusion of player agency. This definition describes "play as repetitive encapsulation of the self by the game [which] feeds the rhetoric of the centrality of the self" (Sutton-Smith, 2001, p. 183).

50 Tanenbaum and Tanenbaum (2010) explained that speech act theory "categorizes an utterance in terms of its illocutionary point, with each kind of point entailing different commitments or attempting to achieve different goals" (p. 13).

51 This is distinct from *influence theory,* in which "the system went beyond simply managing the expectations of the player, and instead used psychological manipulation to attempt to control the actions of the player, without her knowledge" in order to determine whether or not there is a disconnect between players' "cognitive experience of 'being in control' and the actual degree of control allotted to the player" (Tanenbaum & Tanenbaum, 2010, p. 16). This approach includes an analysis of the ways in which games may train players to have certain expectations of interaction and provides a means of looking at how experiences of interactive media shape social processes.

52 The media and communications industries "tend to monopolize control of the mnemotechnical archive by which the material practices and experiences of the past are stored and passed down as culture, heritage, and tradition" (Crogan, 2011, p. 31). Computer and video games, as entertainment, rely on "providing at least the illusion of a suspension of the practices and routines that go with the implementation of technoscientifically produced and regulated productivity...in modern capitalist society," but this "suspension is no doubt always circumscribed in carefully regulated regimes of commodification" (Crogan, 2011, p. 34–35).

53 Crogan (2011) described the influence of this shift in terms of Gonzalo Frasca's argument about the future of media forms: "their future is tied to the fact that simulation deals in a futural temporal mode of user (player) engagement; a simulation, unlike narrative and drama, 'is the form of the future" (p. 143). Simulations address what *may* happen (future), which is distinct from narrative (past) or drama/theater (present). Interactive digital game systems enable this movement toward simulation, and so the relationship between the computer/console and the ideologies it shares plays a role in, but is not the whole of, this medium's influence.

References

Bateson, G. (1955). A theory of play and phantasy. *Psychiatric Research Reports,* 2, 39–51.

Beach, W. (2000). Inviting collaborations in stories about a woman. *Language in Society,* 29, 379–407.

Beavis, C., & Charles, C. (2007). Would the "real" girl gamer please stand up? Gender, LAN-cafés and the reformulation of the "girl" gamer. *Gender and Education,* 19(6), 691–705.

Birkland, T. A., & Lawrence, R. G. (2009). Media framing and policy change after Columbine. *American Behavioral Scientist,* 52(10), 1405–1425.

Bordo, S. (1999). *The male body: A new look at men in public and in private.* New York, NY: Farrar, Straus and Giroux.

Brown, L. M. (1999). *Raising their voices: The politics of girls' anger.* Cambridge, MA: Harvard University Press.

Burns, R. & Crawford, C. (1999). School shootings, the media, and public fear: Ingredients for a moral panic. *Crime, Law and Social Change,* 32(2), 147–168.

Butler, J. (1990). *Gender trouble: Feminism and the subversion of identity.* New York, NY: Routledge.

Butler, J. (1993). *Bodies that matter: On the discursive limits of "sex."* New York, NY: Routledge.

Carnagey, N. L., Anderson, C. A., & Bushman, B. J. (2007). The effect of video game violence on physiological desensitization to real-life violence. *Journal of Experimental Social Psychology, 43*(3), 489–496.

Cassell, J., & Jenkins, H. (1998). *From Barbie to Mortal Kombat: Gender and computer games*. Cambridge, MA: MIT Press.

Cline, V. B., Croft, R. G., & Courrier, S. (1973). Desensitization of children to television violence. *Journal of Personality and Social Psychology, 27*(3), 360–365.

Clough, P. T., & Halley, J. (2007). *The affective turn: Theorizing the social*. Durham, NC: Duke University Press.

Craig, S. (1992). *Men, masculinity, and the media*. Thousand Oaks, CA: Sage Publications.

Crogan, P. (2011). *Gameplay mode: War, simulation, and technoculture*. Minneapolis, MN: University of Minnesota Press.

Derné, S. (2002). Globalization and the reconstitution of local gender arrangements. *Men and Masculinities, 5*(2), 144–164.

Dines, G., & Humez, J. M. (2011). *Gender, race, and class in media: A critical reader*. Thousand Oaks, CA: Sage Publications.

Duggan, L. (1993). The trials of Alice Mitchell: Sensationalsim, sexology, and the lesbian subject in turn-of-the-century America. *Signs, 18*(4), 791–814.

Farquhar, J. C, & Wasylkiw, L. (2007). Media images of men: Trends and consequences of body conceptualization. *Psychology of Men & Masculinity, 8*(3), 145–160.

Ferguson, C. J., Smith, S., Miller-Stratton, H., Fritz, S., & Heinrich, E. (2008). Aggression in the laboratory: Problems with the validity of the modified Taylor Competitive Reaction Time Test as a measure of aggression in media violence studies. *Journal of Aggression, Maltreatment & Trauma, 17*(1), 118–132.

Feshbach, S., & Singer, R. D. (1971). *Television and aggression*. San Francisco, CA: Jossey-Bass Inc.

Funk, J. B., Baldacci, H. B., Pasold, T., & Baumgardner, J. (2004). Violence exposure in real-life, video games, television, movies, and the internet: Is there desensitization? *Journal of Adolescence, 27*(1), 23–39.

Furth, H. G. (1967). Concerning Piaget's view on thinking and symbol formation. *Child Development, 38*(3), 819–826.

Gee, J. P. (2008). Being a lion and being a soldier: Learning and games. In J. Coiro, M. Knobel, C. Lankshear, & D. J. Leu (Eds.), *The handbook of research on new literacies* (p. 1023–1036). New York, NY: Erlbaum/Taylor & Francis Group.

Hammack, P. L. (2008). Narrative and the cultural psychology of identity. *Personality and Social Psychology Review: An Official Journal of the Society for Personality and Social Psychology, Inc., 12*(3), 222–247.

Hargrave, A. M., & Livingstone, S. M. (2009). *Harm and offence in media content: A review of the evidence* (2nd ed.). Chicago, IL: Intellect Books.

Hargreaves, D. A., & Tiggemann, M. (2009). Muscular ideal media images and men's body image: Social comparison processing and individual vulnerability. *Psychology of Men & Masculinity, 10*(2), 109–119.

Hatchell, H. (2006). Masculinities and violence: Interruption of hegemonic discourses in an English classroom. *Discourse: Studies in the Cultural Politics of Education, 27*(3), 383–397.

Hayles, N. K. (1999). *How we became posthuman: Virtual bodies in cybernetics, literature, and informatics.* Chicago, IL: University Of Chicago Press.

Hinojosa, R. (2010). Doing hegemony: Military, men, and constructing a hegemonic masculinity. *The Journal of Men's Studies, 18*(2), 179–194.

Hobza, C. L., & Rochlen, A. B. (2009). Gender role conflict, drive for muscularity, and the impact of ideal media portrayals on men. *Psychology of Men & Masculinity, 10*(2), 120–130.

Hobza, C. L, Walker, K. E., Yakushko, O., & Peugh, J. L. (2007). What about men? Social comparison and the effects of media images on body and self-esteem. *Psychology of Men & Masculinity, 8*(3), 161–172.

Horkheimer, M., & Adorno, T. W. (2002). *Dialectic of enlightenment: Philosophical fragments* (E. Jephcott, Trans.). Stanford, CA: Stanford University Press.

Jenson, J., & de Castell, S. (2010). Gender, simulation, and gaming: Research review and redirections. *Simulation & Gaming, 41*(1), 51–71.

Johnson, P. J., McCreary, D. R., & Mills, J. S. (2007). Effects of exposure to objectified male and female media images on men's psychological well-being. *Psychology of Men & Masculinity, 8*(2), 95–102. doi:10.1037/1524-9220.8.2.95.

Kang, M. (2011). *Sublime dreams of living machines: The Automaton in the European imagination.* Cambridge, MA: Harvard University Press.

Keller, S. N., & Brown, J. D. (2002). Media interventions to promote responsible sexual behavior. *Journal of Sex Research, 39*(1), 67–72.

Kimmel, M. (1996). *Manhood in America: A cultural history.* New York, NY: The Free Press.

Kimmel, M. (2008). *Guyland: The perilous world where boys become men.* New York, NY: Harper Collins.

Klinger, L. J., Hamilton, J. A., & Cantrell, P. J. (2001). Children's perceptions of aggressive and gender-specific content in toy commercials. *Social Behavior & Personality: An International Journal, 29*(1), 11–20.

Morrison, T. G., & Halton, M. (2009). Buff, tough, and rough: Representations of muscularity in action motion pictures. *Journal of Men's Studies, 17*(1), 57–74.

Murray, J. H. (1998). *Hamlet on the holodeck: The future of narrative in cyberspace.* Cambridge, MA: MIT Press.

Newman, J. (2002). In search of the videogame player: The lives of Mario. *New Media & Society, 4*(3), 405–422.

Parasecoli, F. (2005). Feeding hard bodies: Food and masculinities in men's fitness magazines. *Food and Foodways, 13*(1–2), 17–37.

Pasquinelli, E. (2006). The role of expectations in the believability of mediated interactions. *ENACTIVE, 6*, 201–203.

Pasquinelli, E. (2009). The illusion of reality: Cognitive aspects and ethical drawbacks. In C. Wankel & S. Malleck (Eds.), *Emerging ethical issues of life in virtual worlds* (p. 197–215). Charlotte, NC: Information Age Publishing.

Piaget, J. (1962). *Play, dreams and imitation in childhood.* New York, NY: W.W. Norton.

Phillips, D. A. (2005). Reproducing normative and marginalized masculinities: Adolescent male popularity and the outcast. *Nursing Inquiry, 12*(3), 219–230.

Power, M. R. (2009). Video games and a culture of conflict. *Journal of Children and Media, 3,* 90–94.

Rice, J., & O'Gorman, M. (Eds.). (2008). *New media/new methods: The academic turn from literacy to electracy.* Anderson, SC: Parlor Press.

Rosenblum, K. E., & Travis, T. (2008). *The meaning of difference: American constructions of race, sex and gender, social class, sexual orientation, and disability.* New York, NY: McGraw-Hill.

Schott, G. R., & Horrell, K. R. (2000). Girl gamers and their relationship with the gaming culture. *Convergence: The International Journal of Research into New Media Technologies, 6*(4), 36–53.

Seyama, J., & Nagayama, R. S. (2007). The uncanny valley: Effect of realism on the impression of artificial human faces. *Presence: Teleoperators and Virtual Environments, 16*(4), 337–351.

Shannon, C., & Weaver. W. (1963). *The mathematical theory of communication.* Champaign, IL: University of Illinois.

Soulliere, D. M., & Blair, J. A. (2006). Muscle-mania: The male body ideal in professional wrestling. *International Journal of Men's Health, 5*(3), 268–286.

Stewart, L., Cooper, P., Stewart, A., & Friedley, S. (2003). *Communication and gender* (4th ed.). London, UK: Pearson.

Sutton-Smith, B. (1966). Piaget on play: A critique. *Psychological Review, 73*(1), 104–110.

Sutton-Smith, B. (2001). *The ambiguity of play.* Cambridge, MA: Harvard University Press.

Tanenbaum, K., & Tanenbaum, J. (2010). Agency as commitment to meaning: Communicative competence in games. *Digital Creativity, 21*(1), 11–17.

Tylka, T. L., & Calogero, R. M. (2011). Expose the illusions, crack the codes: Contextualizing.

visual media to mold a new reality. *Sex Roles, 65*(7–8), 461–468.

Van Dijk, T. A. (2006). Ideology and discourse analysis. *Journal of Political Ideologies, 11*(2), 115–140.

Van Zoonen, L. (1994). *Feminist media studies.* Thousand Oaks, CA: Sage Publications.

Walton, C., Coyle, A., & Lyons, E. (2004). Death and football: An analysis of men's talk about emotions. *British Journal of Social Psychology, 43*(3), 401–416.

Weber, B. R. (2006). What makes the man? Television makeovers, made-over masculinity, and male body image. *International Journal of Men's Health, 5*(3), 287–306.

Wertsch, J. V. (1984). The zone of proximal development: Some conceptual issues. *New Directions for Child and Adolescent Development, 1984*(23), 7–18.

Wood, J. T. (2011). *Gendered lives: Communication, gender, and culture* (10th ed.). Boston, MA: Wadsworth.

6 Reflective Research

When we play, we engage fully and intensely with life and its contents. Play bores through boredom in order to reach the deep truth of ordinary things.

—Ian Bogost (2016)

6.1 Layers of Meaning

Synthesis of previously discreet theoretical approaches to interactive media study yields a more complete means of addressing questions about the influences of video game play on individuals. The term *ergodic ontogeny* is suggested to capture the experience of individuals' personal self-identification and ideological development as a result of play experiences drawing on key themes of narratology, ludology, and ergodics. Previous dichotomies, such as ludic vs. narrative or player vs. performer, are useful and necessary but act as supporting points for breaking down aspects of interactive media experience. The idea that analyses must include only one or the other is limiting and entirely ignores the complex, dialogic nature of new media literacy in favor of maintaining traditional disciplinary boundaries.

Players' experiences engage multiple aspects of interactive digital game play simultaneously, and these influences must be considered as a whole. The interview data provided in chapters three, four, and five is in no way comprehensive of all elements of interactive play experience but do provide data from which initial, basic themes emerged and serve as starting points for more comprehensive and interdisciplinary approaches. This chapter will reaffirm the benefits of social scientific methods, such as interviews and discourse analysis, posit preferred new directions of study, and reflexively address the methodological, analytical, and compositional aspects of this project as a whole.

The valuing of social scientific, qualitative data must be addressed, because quantitative methods are often hailed for their repeatability and mathematical specificity. Qualitative methods are possibly less well understood in terms of their merits. Interviewing techniques are varied, each with their own benefits and limitations.[1] Interview data provide personal accounts of experience but can only be as accurate as the information respondents choose to report or are able to remember. The potential for false associations/memories is important to keep in mind, but incorrect memory is never reported as surely or descriptively as memories of which people are certain (Weiss, 2004). The interview process is a joint venture between the interviewer and the respondent, and building rapport is a critical goal. In-depth interviews provide a depth of information regarding participants' real and virtual lived experiences. Individual interviews include time for more personal reflections on the part of the research participant without concerns of being interrupted by others or being overlooked (as might be the case for less outgoing/social participants in group interviews or focus group settings). Personal insights and individual reflections are an essential component of research, often best used with mixed methods. Interview data is the narrative that supports and augments other data, without which the story of research cannot exist.

Patton (2002) supported qualitative data including interviews and observations and explained the qualitative research process in terms of "voluminous raw data," such as interview responses and field notes, that are "organized into readable narrative descriptions. ... The themes, patterns, understandings, and insights that emerge from fieldwork and subsequent analysis are the fruit of qualitative inquiry" (p. 5). It is with this in mind that the thematic content of each chapter emerged from patterns in interview data and analysis/insights into their meaning. Researchers with inside knowledge and perspectives of the groups they study have many advantages but must also keep their biases in mind when reporting.[2]

Generating and reaffirming components of ergodic ontogeny, as evidenced by player discourse, and situating these themes in relation to academic conceptions of interactive media require a grounded theory that is "inductively generated from fieldwork, that is, theory that emerges from the researcher's observations and interviews out in the real world rather than in the laboratory or the academy" (Patton, 2002, p. 11). The "credibility of qualitative methods, therefore, hinges to a great extent on the skill, competence, and rigor of the person doing fieldwork—as well as things going on in a person's life" (Patton, 2002, p. 14).[3] The researcher must be close to the people and situations under investigation to understand the depth of information shared through this methodology. The interview data from the previous chapters is supplemented with discourse and pragmatic analyses as well as knowledge acquired through my lived experience[4] and ethnographic observation.

The present data set may be analyzed through a variety of means beyond those incorporated here. Details of players' talk were analyzed for explicit instances of broader trends in this purposive sample.[5]

Gee (2010) argued against a strict or static approach to discourse analysis[6] and stressed the importance of the *influence* and *action* of language. The ways players speak throughout the interview process imply power relations, cultural and political persuasions, access to academic or other professional discourses, and many other potential signifiers. In analyzing linguistic data,[7] the researcher must attend to the co-construction of socioculturally situated identities, social languages, and participants' abilities to build meaning in narrative.[8] Though selected to illustrate key themes of ergodic ontogeny, the interview data in this book can teach much more about the people who were interviewed depending on one's analytical frame.

Bucholtz (1999) provided a framework for investigating language use as an expression and construction of identity and social practices and explained that communities of practice describe identities as the result of positive and negative identity practices rather than as fixed social categories, as in the speech-community model.[9] Non-linguistic practices may carry important linguistic information, and sociolinguistic analysis must examine multiple levels of language simultaneously.[10] Linguistic and social practices at the local level reproduce existing social arrangements. Bucholtz (1999)[11] argued that by recognizing practice, defined as the social projects of participants, as the *motivating context* for linguistic interaction, the theory of the community of practice makes activity central to sociolinguistic analysis. The *speech community* model understands language as fundamentally disembodied (detachable from the physicality of speakers), but the *community of practice* model reincorporates language into the physical self, echoing Bourdieu's concept of *hexis*.[12]

Analysis and coding of information gathered through the research process raise concerns about the validity of these practices. How can we know whether the researcher's interpretations are valid? How can the complexity of experience truly be evaluated at all, and how can that evaluation be adequately conveyed within the limits of academic research? Clarke (2005) explored concepts, themes, and analytics emerging from the research process and the stages of research that lead to these perspectives. Moya and Hames-Garcia (2000), on the other hand, argued for positivism that recognizes its flaws. My own analysis lies somewhere between the two: hyper-aware of potential subjectivities but attempting to provide meaningful and authentic ideas while recognizing my limitations. We are all embedded within our own social and epistemological positionings, which must be acknowledged.[13]

Mani (1990) described this concept as the "revolt of the particular against that masquerading as the general, of what Donna Haraway has called 'situated' as against 'disembodied knowledges,'" which has "brought to the fore theoretical and political questions regarding positionality and identity" (p. 392).[14] Small samples of interview data, like those provided for detailed analysis in this project, are purposive samples that cannot be generalized but do provide *deep* insights and recognize situated knowledges (Adler & Adler, 2002). For example, male interview participants accepted violent themes in entertainment but did not feel comfortable linguistically expressing their own violent actions or emotions. Mechanisms for framing interactive play experiences were often located within play contexts as children and young adults.[15] Participants expressed the desire to deny any connection between themes in their play and work, but their speech displayed a relationship between the two. These specific experiences cannot be generalized to all players of video games. Yet, we have gained insights into the ways in which some males in the United States internalize social expectations of masculine identity and reaffirm cultural ideologies that have relevance in real life through such play activities.

Themes of masculinity informed the direction of analysis and provided the foundation for talking about interactive media influence due to the propensity of game designers to cater to this assumed audience and the popular discourse that links violent interactive media content with aggression, masculinity, and competitive play. Russ (1972) suggested that "our literature is not about women. It is not about women and men equally. It is by and about men" (p. 200).[16] Despite some shifts in media over the years since her writing, the themes of modern media content still often reflect this trend. Russ (1972) proclaimed that "culture is male" (p. 201), and narrative plots—Aristotle's mythos—"are dramatic embodiments of what a culture believes to be true—or what it would like to be true—or what it is mortally afraid may be true...which includes not women but images of women" (p. 202).

Russ (1972) was writing about literature and scripts in the traditional, text-based, paper-bound sense. Yet, the idea of *bildungsroman* (that a novel is about the moral and psychological growth of the main character) can certainly be borrowed from literary criticism and applied to interactive media narratives, as long as the necessary distinctions between these media are understood.[17] Myths are culturally available (acceptable) patterns[18] that dictate most narrative. Mass media content, for fear of losing its audience or declining sales in the modern cut-throat capitalist economy, does not veer far into the territory of underrepresented voices or stories. Therefore, to address the dominant forms of this medium, it is necessary to address masculinity head-on, and proceed from that starting point to eventually broach other discourses from other players.

6.2 Limited Identities for Unexpected Players

Many studies focus on a single aspect of video game influence and establish valid pieces of the puzzle. Meta-analyses of interactive media literature show that individual research results are varied and often contradictory. More researchers are needed to pull data from multiple resources, combine findings, and posit results informed across and between disciplines with a critical eye to how such results operate in cultural terms while keeping in mind their own personal subjectivities. This is not an insignificant task. Individual research findings (such as those included here) are essential as interactive media theory reaches the levels of scholarship of past media forms.

Martin (2012) explored youth identity within the MMORPG *World of Warcraft* (*WoW*) and recognized identities as "combinations of the participants' skill and level in the game, as well as their play style" (p. 384). Massively multiplayer online role-playing games allow players to choose their character's identity to a large degree and to choose which goals to pursue at what time to progress through the virtual environment. Martin (2012) found that *WoW* players between the ages of 14 and 18 years exhibited "identities in action" through their use of technology; they created "multifaceted identity processes that are constantly in flux, just as their information resources are in flux...Their identity production is bricolage; it is a process rather than being fixed and static" and bridges "their virtual and physical world" (p. 389). Significantly, this is a report of their personal identities, not the identities of the avatars within the game world, which supports the layered comprehensive identity construction resulting from ergodic ontogeny.

Bricker and Bell (2012) described the "learning practices embedded in the structural nexus of [an individual] youth's gaming" and examined "associated issues of learning and identity" situated in contexts such as school experiences (p. 883). Farrar, Krcmar, and McGloin (2013) further analyzed player identification by turning to visual representations on the screen and player perceptions of these human forms. They found that "less human-looking targets were perceived as less human," that "the more experience someone had playing violent games, the less violent they perceived the stimulus game to be," that "men were more physically aggressive than women," and that perceptions of aggression, whether toward humans or not, generated the most aggressive responses (Farrar et al., 2013, p. 300).

A recent trend is the study of *alternate* game audiences (almost anyone other than adolescent boys). Talk about video game habits provided in the previous chapters demonstrated dissonance with masculine discourses that are common to entertainment media forms. Recognition of this disjuncture has trickled (to a limited extent in mainstream mass-produced video game titles, but to a greater degree in indie games) to the attention of developers who are beginning to acknowledge a desire for narratives beyond traditional machismo. This shift involves the consideration of non-traditional gamer audiences.

Enevold and Hagstrom (2009), for example, discussed mothers (usually stay-at-home moms, but not exclusively) as gamers.[19] Cries of the

threat of gaming addiction and violent behavioral responses to interactive digital play are becoming more nuanced as discourses change
based on increases in home console use. Enevold and Hagstrom (2009)
noted "an increasing attention among games researchers to players in
addition to the games themselves," and asserted that "ethnologists have
a particular methodological edge and a role to fulfill as games research
more and more means studying games in relation to gamers, society and
political economy and not only the game itself" (p. 2). Since the release
of the Nintendo Wii, and arguably to a certain extent with home consoles beforehand, there are an ever-expanding number of home gamers
of various ages playing games with a vast array of subject matter.

The study of women, specifically mothers, as a unique demographic is
of particular interest because it contradicts the stereotype of the traditional gamer, especially considering the fact that games take time to complete (non-trivial effort), a serious investment in the modern era. Enevold
and Hagstrom (2009) argued that "a mother who plays computer games
challenges cultural norms, claiming time for an unproductive activity
only for her, acts in contradiction to what the concept of 'mother' implies...Games, seen as personal time-consuming pleasures, may cause
conflict" (p. 7). Categorizing games as unproductive is clearly limited
and ignores the identification and mental stimulation that keep players
engaged. Shifts in player demographics[20] necessarily influence the games
that will be made and the methods through which designers will attempt
player/character identification.

The ways in which games depict certain groups as either primary
or secondary characters in a story has an effect, even if moderated by
external experiences, on players' perceptions of that group. Certain
demographics are over-represented and others are lacking[21] which,
"according to social identity theory (Tajfel, 1978)...is a direct signal...
that [some groups] are relatively unimportant and powerless compared
to more heavily present groups" (Williams, Martins, Consalvo, & Ivory,
2009, p. 828). Ultimately, the blame for representation patterns is placed
on developer demographics as well as marketer's perceptions of gamer
audiences. The disparity between the people playing video games, an
increasingly diverse group, and those represented in its narratives is a
factor that may inhibit player identification and certainly alters the connections players have to interactive digital experiences.

6.3 The Physical Effects of Interactive Play

The data gathered and presented here are but a single lens through which
to explore ergodic ontogeny, serving as an example of one piece of a
puzzle and helping to establish themes that may appear via other analytical approaches as well. A different and useful direction of interactive
media research is collaboration with psychologists and neuroscientists

to incorporate functional magnetic resonance imaging (fMRI)—a scan of brain activation—into discussions of media influence. Anderson, Jennings Bryant, Murray, Rivkin, and Zillman (2009) referenced three studies using magnetic resonance imaging to record brain activation in relation to media effects, which recorded activations while adult male research participants played interactive digital games with varied content. Anderson et al. (2009) described fMRI as a "remarkable technology [that] has rapidly spawned numerous techniques with which to study both brain structure and function in a quantitative—yet noninvasive—fashion" (p. 2). Difficulties inherent in fMRI research include potential "failure to appreciate the difficulties of working in collaboration with scientists and scholars from very diverse fields," gaining access to "the right professional facilities," and the very real concerns regarding time-consuming processes of "data analysis and interpretation" (Anderson et al., 2009, p. 3). When situations arise in which these factors align, then evocative, efficient research can lead to incredible new insights.

Mathiak and Weber (2006) collaborated with researchers in Germany and the United States and found, with experienced gamers between the ages of 18 and 26 years, playing a FPS game during fMRI showed that an "activation pattern reflects brain-environment interactions rather than stimulus responses as observed in classical experimental designs" (p. 948). Granek, Gorbet, and Sergio (2010) found "additional prefrontal cortex activity in experienced video gamers planning for complex eye-hand coordination tasks that are distinct from actual video-game play" (p. 187). Gong et al. (2015) reported enhanced functional activity and gray matter in action video game players of advanced skill. Interactive digital play changes the way brains work,[22] based on these findings, but does not necessarily have specific stimulation effects related to media content.

The difficulty in working across and between disciplines is all the more reason to shift disciplinary notions of academia to forge connections between the sciences and the humanities. We must embrace this challenge and collaborate effectively with a shared goal of deeper, more meaningful, and accurate data gathering and analysis.[23] Triangulating conclusions across/within multiple disciplines is the only way to achieve a complete understanding of the influences of interactive media. Ulmer suggested that "the new technologies of photography, film, video and computers transform what we call 'thinking'" (Rice & O'Gorman, 2008, p. 48), a shift that may be displayed physically in fMRI results.[24]

Virtual experiential learning is useful compensation for people who have difficulty with traditional literacy and also suggestive of a new electronic literacy.[25] Multimodal literacy tasks may aid in the use of compensatory neural networks as an effective means of engaging participants, learners, or audiences more fully. Concepts of postindustrial modernity led to the idea that not merely play and games, but life itself should be fun.[26] This raises the question of whether or not there is still, and if there should be, a distinction between play and reality. Has ludic identification and gamification changed the way people interpret information in a fundamental way?[27] Are attention spans shortening or changing? Has electracy taken the place of traditional literacy? Are there physical shifts in brain activity regarding cognition of digital and interactive texts and the influence of their thematic content? Functional magnetic resonance (fMRI) imaging may be a necessary tool for addressing some of these questions and may help bridge the gap between sciences and humanities.

6.4 Reflexivity

There are a number of essential considerations regarding the process of conducting this research: analyzing the data, writing the text, and the rationale for including this self-reflective analysis. Reflexivity provides valuable insights into the relations of power present at each stage of the research process as well as the assumptions and perceptions brought to the field by the researchers' own position.[28] Reflexivity involves the crucial consideration that fieldwork, analysis, and writing do not occur in a vacuum and that no individual is free from influence of the Other.[29] All writing is a construction—our version or telling of the world (Emerson, Fretz, & Shaw, 1995). Writing is a persuasive activity in which the writer shares information through a personal lens of experience and knowing.[30] The writing of interview questions, for example, reflected knowledge gathered through extensive research of new media literature, personal experiences of interactive digital play, and growing up with the technology of in-home consoles. Some interview questions were revised, and some omitted entirely, to avoid potentially making participants feel uncomfortable or suggesting thematic connections that seemed natural to me, but were not necessarily true for all players. Participants bring certain expectations as to what it means to take part in *research* and bring their own assumptions as to what the interviewer might be looking for (placing the interviewer in a position of additional authority or power in the interview setting).[31]

The process of transcribing interviews is similarly complex.[32] It is a process that involves decisions on the part of the transcriber as to interpretation and representation, even when attempting to be as detailed, comprehensive, and objective as possible. My choice to transcribe in a naturalized style was the result of a principal interest in the content of the talk rather than the mode (so it was less important to record specific accents or pronunciations). Only later did I search emergent themes for more detailed pragmatic analysis of specific selections of text. At that time, nuances were transcribed, such as laughter, changing tone of voice for comedic or other effect, and long (between 2 to 4 second) pauses. In these ways, transcription and certainly ethnographic analysis overall are not "transparent and unproblematic records of scientific research but...creative and politicized documents in which the researcher as author is fully implicated" (Bucholtz, 2000, p. 1440). The content of interviews determined the coding of data, but coding was also dependent on my personal decisions. Themes reflected the questions asked of the interviewees, again supporting the leading nature of interview research. However, the semi-structured individual interview process provided opportunities for a mutual building of conversational data that ultimately yielded meaningful insights, even without definite generalizability.

Reflexivity requires that the researcher examine how his or her "research agenda and assumptions, subject location(s), personal beliefs, and emotions enter into their research" (Hsiung, 2008, p. 212). This process cannot be learned passively and requires repeated practice to learn how to engage in active self-examination. Each choice in a project is constructed through the researcher's own lens of experience, context, and background. As a nearly lifelong player of video games, years of non-academic participant observation influenced (though often silent or implied) all of the analysis within this project.[33]

Feminist methodologies situate the researcher as an active participant in the research process.[34] Therefore, it is necessary to explain the reasons behind my methodological choices. The complexity of numerous voices and hierarchies present in socio-cultural situations requires a constant process of evaluation and re-evaluation of best practices and a conscientious awareness of the influence of research on others. For example, the term *gender* has numerous and mixed connotations. Distinguished from the physical sexual characteristics of an individual, I use the term to denote the culturally ascribed qualities of an individual's appearance, behavior, use of language, or other defining characteristics.[35] Reflexivity and transparency in writing require authors to project what assumptions might be made about their work and position their contributions as fairly as possibly within the realm of current understandings. All communication is biased in one way or another. Again, we must provide and explain our situated knowledges while incorporating multiple voices and perspectives, keeping in mind the particular moment in time in which research, writing, and expression takes place.[36]

Additionally, consciousness-raising is an important component of reflexivity.[37] Fonow and Cook (1991) argued that exposing hidden powers is an innate part of research, which supports Collins' (2000) valuing of the researcher's position as an *outsider within,* who is therefore more likely to challenge claims of insiders in a given group and to identify and acknowledge discrepancies between insider accounts and her own experiences.[38] These elements of critical research are reflected in the report of masculine discourses that are either mocked or disavowed by some men—a population not commonly associated with underrepresentation or oppression.

Issues of research ethics are all the more important if we assume that all action results in some form of call to or shift in consciousness. For example, if power differentials are eased between researcher and participant, as they ideally were in this case, then I must strictly adhere to guarantees of confidentiality.[39] Working with participants to co-construct meaning opens a dialogue that can be emotionally evocative, and maintaining their anonymity protects them, as much as possible, from vulnerabilities.[40] Vulnerability, similar to considerations of emotion as a meaningful theme in culture, has often been avoided.[41] Emotions[42] are some of the "ways in which we engage actively and even construct the world. They have both 'mental' and 'physical' aspects" (Jaggar, 1989, p. 382). The interview data presented here certainly supports a hesitation on the part of male interviewees to discuss emotional responses and a guarded interaction when broaching such topics.

The linguistic data included in this book provides examples of men defining other men in terms of their masculinity, which takes the form of talk about body type, self-discipline, martial ability, and hypermasculinity. Hinojosa (2010) explained that "men construct a hegemonically oriented masculinity by symbolically constructing masculine hierarchies in which they situate themselves on top" (p. 179) through expressions of hegemonic, subordinated, marginalized, complicit, or resistance/protest masculinities.[43] Grounded theory generates insight based on the researcher's positionality as informed by linguistic data provided by participants.[44] In this way, the process of working with coded data relies on a constant comparative method of both gathering and analyzing data.

To discuss qualitative or quantitative methods as non-gendered entities ignores inherent characteristics of culture, academia, and personal identity. It is important, in that case, to maintain a critical awareness of the effects of hierarchies of power in the research setting that might influence the information collected, the experiences and future lives of participants in research, and the work of the researcher. It is crucial to include multiple voices, including those that are traditionally underrepresented, in any attempt to get at a more fully aware version of reality. Male and female writers are viewed differently when writing about subjects that have gendered cultural assumptions (Lorde, 1984). Authors are judged not only according to the present social structure, but also by the structures that have been built up over long periods of marginalization. This issue is especially relevant when discussing gendered issues such as identity, whether masculine or feminine.

Historical approaches to research trace why particular scientific or socially based questions are asked at certain periods of time. Researchers must "view objectivity as a 'particular and specific embodiment,'" rather than as a "false vision promising transcendence of all limits and responsibility (Haraway 1988, 582)" (Bhavnani, 1993, p. 67). My approach to interviewing, transcribing, coding, and analyzing information is influenced by these considerations in terms of my own sense of moral and ethical codes of conduct in research and writing.[45] As discussed in the preface of this book, knowledge and writing are situated experiences (historically, culturally, and in many other ways). The arguments put forth in these pages tell of my work during the years of research that led to my original formulation of the concept of ergodic ontogeny. It is a start. This work must be continued, updated, and expanded.

The foregrounding of personal experience as a primary source of knowledge is sometimes criticized, because "granting priority to experience... can lead to a 'politics of identity'"; no personal experience can cover all human experience, yet "insight into and appropriation of experience is critical" (Gottfried, 1996, p. 5). There must be a connection between theory, research, and experience. Voice and agency are both important, but do not stand on their own. The reliance on participants for experiential knowledge must be handled fairly. My discussion of player identity is informed by this critical lens; participants' discourse was collected through a digital recorder (as opposed to note taking or memory or other less reliable methods), coded according to its literal content for thematic trends, and then analyzed according to pragmatic discourse. Readers' understandings of this data, however, are always framed in terms of my analysis as the author and my selection of data for inclusion.[46]

Researchers and participants must question one another's actions and perceptions.[47] There is no single procedure for production of a single *true* story.[48] We must embrace a plurality that acknowledges the importance of difference in collaboration across disciplines.[49] Rice and O'Gorman (2008)[50] asserted that "to develop a new aesthetics of new media, we should pay as much attention to cultural history as to the computer's unique new possibilities to generate, organize, manipulate, and distribute data" (p. 10); theory is not the "content or object" of study but is a creative act, a "generative poetics" (p. 22).[51] The way in which this book is structured reflects these ideas: building from one idea (between disciplines) to the next, then moderating those conceptions with interview data gathered directly from participants, valuing individual expression and insight through pragmatic discourse analysis, and also incorporating videos, enabling links,[52] and providing self-referential opportunities for critique.[53] This text, however, is not ergodic, just e-literate. Even the most prominent critical theorists almost always operate in text-based media due to conventional ideas of knowledge legitimacy (the published book).

6.5 In Conclusion

This book supports the interconnectedness of media, culture, identity development, and society. "Cultural and social factors shape technology far more than technology shapes culture" (Jenkins, 2010). Cultural productions are signs and rituals that serve the function of establishing "a new direction...[and] contribute to the progress of modernity by presenting new combinations of cultural elements" (MacCannell, 1976, p. 26).[54] Continued study of interactive media influence must accommodate shifts in what new media means for the changing face of a capitalist nation: a forum for public voice, new levels of accountability to the public/players, and an awareness of cultural and personal identity development. Ergodic ontogeny explores ideological and identity development and the nature of socialization as it changes due to advances in new interactive digital media content and media forms.

Interactive media play experiences lead to internalization of game content, ludic interactivity, and character identification in ways that are more immersive and affective than past media. The use of the words *play* and *game* to imply a trivialization of action or intent, a wasting of time, or a lack of sincerity or seriousness of expression is dominant. Yet, when situations arise for which other social factors provide insufficient explanation, *video games* often become the focus of intense criticism. The influence of virtual realities and immersive digital play that harkens from a tradition of simulation for training purposes is hotly contested and requires complex layers of inquiry rather than single lenses of analysis.

The participants in this study outwardly denied a connection between play/fantasy and reality but linguistically connected these experiences while expressing unexpected rationalizations and emotional responses. Players recognized cultural stereotypes and, although conforming to them regularly, stated their dissatisfaction with such expectations and yearned for a more balanced sociocultural playing field. Prominent themes in discourses of gaming, in relation to identity and ideology, included heroic protective discourse, the use of games as outlets for aggression, experiences of emotional catharsis even in mundane aspects of play, and the acting out of social roles in virtual environments. Players internalized interactive digital play experiences in ways that are informed by their knowledge of the relationship between games and reality. By establishing key themes of narrative, immersion, identification, and the complex differences between the virtual and the real as the foundations for ergodic ontogeny, future research may draw on this approach to a seemingly elusive developmental process in order to address discrepancies between common conceptions of video games' influence and players' experiences.

The personal development resulting from interactive digital media gaming beyond, yet due to, play experiences is crucial as technology reaches increasing percentages of the world population. An accurate, authentic analysis of the influence of interactive media forms requires an interdisciplinary methodological approach that includes a cohesive analysis of games' influence incorporating play theory, ludology, narratology, and ergodic theories. The discourse analysis provided here serves merely as a foundation for themes of ergodic ontogeny that will be further established through future research incorporating linguistic and other qualitative data along with analyses of interactive texts themselves, players' physiological reactions to game experiences as captured through fMRI scans or other means of discerning physical reactions to play, and continued reports from game players, designers, and analysts. This book defines the first emergent themes of ergodic ontogeny for a sample of adult male gamers and affirms the crucial nature of interdisciplinarity in interactive digital media research.

Ergodic ontogeny is the personal mental development resulting from interactive digital media play experiences: the development of a sense of self (moral, ideological, epistemological) that results from new knowledge/experiences through game play in immersive, agentive, virtual environments in which the player is an active agent *influencing* and *being influenced by* play. Ideological and identity construction through interactive digital media, through the internalization of new personal and cultural knowledge, is distinct from, though related to, real-world experience.

Interactive media will increasingly become the vehicle for our cultural narratives, shaping our sense of self and society as other media have done before them. The specific affordances of this new interactive form alter our modes of personal development. Interactive digital media is more than a tool and more than a playful technical improvement on past entertainment practices. My hope is that the perspectives presented in this book will help bridge the gap between academic (often extremely detailed, necessarily nuanced, and at times entirely theoretical) and popular media discussions of video games, open the complexities of interactive digital media scholarship to more and varied readers, and justify directions for future research that value the incredible influence of this form of play.

Notes

1 Weiss (2004) presented a helpful overview of the nature of qualitative interviews, explaining that this method focuses on what is said and done and how the respondent thinks and feels about it. Participants have the opportunity to explain fully the processes leading up to events or experiences, the details of which are gathered in hopes of illuminating why it happened (p. 498).

2 The need for reflexivity is addressed in detail in the final section of this chapter.

3 Qualitative research's primary purpose "is to generate or test theory and contribute to knowledge for the sake of knowledge" (Patton, 2002, p. 10).

4 Reflexive research requires full disclosure of considerations of my own positionality within this research process and analysis, as well as my personal experiences and motivations that inform decisions regarding topics, interview questions, and examples. As a young child in the late 1980s and 1990s, my play practices consisted primarily of imagination and games played with other children, facilitated by toys, stories, fables and rhymes, props, jungle

gyms, or simply verbal make-believe. The common play practices of children in middle-class families on the east coast of the United States during this time were supportive of creativity and invention, yet limited in appropriate (non-violent, non-sexual) content and gendered representations.

5 To provide an even more complete conception of the meanings drawn from this data, future research may build on analysis regarding connections between play and career choice (Cole, 2013).

6 The goal of discourse analysis for Gee (2010) is to explore the relationships between language and practice (doing), which often includes politics (critical discourse analysis).

7 Discourse analysis can be applied to images; the way we understand narrative is relevant regardless of medium. The important difference to keep in mind is the way in which specific media alter our understandings of the text's content according to their means of communication. Gee (2010) noted that humans communicate via symbol systems or systems composed using modalities other than language and even mix other systems with language (p. 194). If we consider images (either still or moving, physical or virtual) as words, breaking them down to their smallest units and exploring the relationships between these units in specific contexts, then a discourse analysis of image is no more susceptible to error than one of spoken or written language that uses words. The same techniques for assuring validity can be applied to both, because, with the exception of the type of unit of analysis, the function of the analysis is exactly the same.

8 Gee (2010) explored the co-construction of socially situated identities in interviews, the same as any other conversation. Differences between interview responses result not only from the particular figured worlds used by the interviewees, but also from the ways in which questions are posed by the interviewer. This is especially important in social research in terms of validity and awareness of how methodology influences results.

9 Bucholtz (1999) described *nerd* identity as not necessarily a stigma imposed by people outside of a group, but often a purposefully chosen alternative to mainstream identities, which is achieved and maintained through language and other social practices.

10 Bucholtz (1999) pointed out that Bourdieu sees the individual as a product of social structure rather than as a free agent and that Certeau sees the individual as more agentive, focusing on investigation as a form of subversion as well as a reproduction of social order. Both Certeau and Bourdieu base such projects in linguistics.

11 Bucholtz (1999) considered the gendered body as the theoretical starting point for research. She wrote about a community of practice of nerd girls, which included both negative and positive identity practices, and examined the phonological and syntactic patterns of self-identified nerds. This community shared many characteristics with traditional audiences of interactive media models, and the enacting of specific social roles could, therefore, be a starting point for yet another lens of analysis to apply to the interview data presented here.

12 The expression of Bourdieu's habitus: predispositions enacted socially.

13 Examples of interactive media content provided in this book are indicative of the types of games that I, personally, am interested in and aware of and are therefore limited in that capacity. I do not consider myself an avid gamer (a helpful distance in my opinion). However, compared to most women my age, it could be argued that I spend a well above average amount of free time engaged in this type of entertainment media practice. This stems from

my early adoption of computer and console games (a product of growing up where I did, when I did, and with access to family members who could afford new technologies) and also from a continued interest and professional association with computer technology more generally. This influenced my willingness to adopt interactive media technology as it has advanced and to value its affordances above past media. After researching social phenomena related to low-budget filmmaking in graduate school and participating in feature-length video productions (DVD releases), I was versed in analysis of the practical aspects of media making and its influences. The logical next step, for me, was to explore narratives that were more emotionally and cognitively evocative than film (video games) due to the increased level of player engagement and senses of agency in the play experience.

14 Mani (1990) revised the politics of location to include the complex historical struggles essential to understanding, referenced Mohanty's (1988) conception of location as a temporality of struggle rather than a fixed term, and supported reflexivity in the research process.

15 Analyses of interview data and theoretical considerations were influenced by my own participation in this media form, and my observation of friends, family, interview participants, and students who played video games. Interactions with interview participants were critically considered in terms of the effects on speech as a result of my being a younger female researcher at the time of our meetings. Rapport was facilitated by my sharing of personal experiences with video games, titles that I enjoy (especially those that I felt might connect to participants' own experiences and add to my credibility as a person who knows enough about games to converse in a sophisticated manner about their insights and play habits) and by maintaining a casual and conversational tone.

16 For example, Susan Koppleman argued that science fiction (a theme common to video game narratives) is white male fiction (Russ, 1972).

17 As already established, borrowing literary terms is often problematic. Applying this concept to game *narrative* specifically helps mediate this concern.

18 Russ (1972) argued that culture is predominantly male-centric/dictated, and also western European.

19 There is some debate as to how to go about studying these so-called nontraditional gamers online and off, but "understanding the ideological underpinnings of *play* is vital to understanding the contexts in which games and gaming exists because they constitute some of the fundamental conditions of games research" (Enevold & Hagstrom, 2009, p. 1–2).

20 Williams et al. (2009) provided a content analysis of 150 games from a single year across nine platforms to explore representations of people in game narratives according to gender, race, and age in comparison to the United States population. Just as in television research, there was over-representation of white, adult males and a systemic under-representation of females, children, and elderly, and of racial diversity. "Because media character demographics and portrayals of social groups may influence players' likelihood of attending to and learning from game characters (Bandura, 1994), as well as players' perceptions of social reality...establishing sound baseline measures of videogame character demographics is a necessary step in applying theories of influence, identity construction, and perceived social reality" (Williams et al., 2009, p. 816–817).

21 Li, Jackson, and Trees' (2008) research on MMORPGs in China addressed responsibilities in real versus online scenarios and explored the influence of game narrative and experience on players in a non-western context.

Li et al. (2008) utilized the "the theory of dialectical contradictions...to examine relationships developed in a Chinese online role-playing game... representing three basic thematic families—integration–separation, expression–nonexpression, and stability–change" (p. 76). Social aspects of online play are often reported as most pleasurable. See Griffiths, Davies, and Chappell (2003) survey of nearly 12,000 players of *Everquest* with 41% supporting responses. Li et al. (2008) explained that graphical environments allow users to be more expressive and sociable, resulting in less emphasis on clear story or narrative structure in these instances. Online play is an important category of interactive digital entertainment with different goals for the relationships developed between players and characters than in single-player gaming. Li et al. (2008) found that "although there may be competing tensions between real-world and online relationships, online and offline relationships do not have the same priority for players. Their offline life is always the primary concern" (p. 95). Their findings support that offline (or out-of-game) realities influence choices made in-game, which is relevant to all forms of interactive digital play. Not only the ability, but the intentional choice, to maintain conscious separation between in-game and non-game realities, especially in MMORPGs that have such strong elements of interpersonal interaction and relationship building, is telling of the extent to which interactive play, narrative-driven or not, may influence players' reality.

22 te Wildt, Rojas, Wedegartner, and Szycik (2010) tested 20 gamers and 20 control participants using fMRI to determine effects of what they considered *excessive play* of interactive media with violent content. te Wildt et al. (2010) found that when "fMRI-scans were performed under presentation of pictures taken from the IAPS...The first-person-shooter players, half of whom fulfilled the criteria of computer game dependency, scored significantly higher (p≤.05) in 4 out of 6 factors of aggressiveness" (p. 779).

23 A kind of technological determinism is at play in the shifts we see regarding digital literacy, and in the ways in which we are capable of investigating these shifts. Ong (1983), for example, argued that literacy moves us away from memory and the personalization of oral culture, but also allows for complexity of thought and maximized theoretical potentials. New media *electracy* is moving knowledge, cultural consumption and production, and socially determined ideologies into the realm of the visual, interactive, and immediate. These concepts of externalized memory provide banks of information that can be made available to later generations. Without thoughtful consideration, however, the mere existence of these vast storage units (online or on external hardware devices) does not instigate intellectual growth. This is not meant to refer necessarily to so-called academic intellectualism, but to a move toward a more authentic understanding of the human experience in modern society. Interaction with technology is shaped by our cultural understandings, and also shapes the ways in which cultural trends form.

24 A pilot study, "An fMRI Study of Interventional Effectiveness: Re-training Dyslexic Students' Neural Pathways to Literacy as a Model for Training Students in New Forms of Electracy" (Saper & Cole) was presented at the Maryland Neuroimaging Retreat in November 2012. The purpose of this study was to research multimodal strategies in compensatory recruitment of frontal and bi-lateral brain regions using fMRI data to trace the emergence of neural circuits for reading, listening, and interacting through electronic literacy. Building on similar work (Eden et al., 1996; Eden & Moats, 2002), this study would explore hypotheses that participants use more parts of their

brain for literacy/exact tasks due to multimodal compensation training and that such activation is similar to non-focused attention, imagining virtual spaces via soundscapes, and interactive navigations tasks. The second hypothesis was that the areas of the brain used/activated for literacy among those trained using mnemonic devices are similar to those used in electronic literacy or electracy. My involvement in this pilot study informed my suggestions for future research and interdisciplinary collaboration posited in this chapter.

25 See Dietz, Jones, Gareau, Zeffiro, and Eden (2005), Eden et al. (1996), Eden and Moats (2002), Landau (2012), and Purcell, Napoliello, and Eden (2011).

26 See MacCannell (1976), among others.

27 Interesting discussions of gamification presented by Gabe Zichermann can be viewed here: http://www.gamification.co/about-gabe-zichermann/.

28 As Roulston (2010) noted, "reflexivity should not be confused with 'reflection,' although the former may involve the latter: while reflection demands thinking about something, it does not require an 'other'" (p. 116).

29 Subjectivity is not simply autobiographical confession, but an intentional and structured approach to positionality.

30 As Kleinman, Copp, and Henderson (1997) discussed, researchers need to be aware of what they know as they come to understand their setting; they must be vulnerable to make mistakes, and realize *everything* is data (even errors in questions or comments).

31 It is important to consider that, in purposive snowball sampling, participants are recommended, often by friends, and might only be participating as a favor.

32 Bucholtz (2000) described transcription as a "practice inherently embedded in relations of power" (p. 1439).

33 My biases were minimized to an extent by maintaining a close reading of the pre-established interview questions during the interview process, though rapport was essential and occasional personal interjections were used to imply my familiarity with the media and concepts participants discussed.

34 The feminist research perspective applies "a critique of each field's biases and distortions" using approaches that "are fundamentally affected by critiques of the ways each field studies women and gender" (Fonow & Cook, 1991, p. 2). My research on gendered discourse and identity applies this level of critique to expectations of both femininity and masculinity.

35 Scott (1986) pointed out that authors "...use 'gender' as a way of referring to the social organization of the relationship between the sexes," but both grammar and language are constantly changing (p. 1053). Mohanty (1988) added that culture plays a key role in the ways in which these representations take shape.

36 Fonow and Cook (1991) reviewed the second wave of feminism and reported finding four main themes: "reflexivity; an action orientation; attention to the affective components of the research; and use of the situation-at-hand" (p. 2). Like Kaplan's (1964) notion of *logic-in-use*, reflexivity is a critical self-attention during the research process to one's own analysis and approach.

37 My previous research focused on film studies; the added level of agency made possible through interactivity changes media research in critical ways. If watching a film may alter personal identify or understanding of how the world works, how does this change once the audience feels a sense of control over the direction of the story? My coursework and guidance in past research fostered a critical concern for reliability, validity, ethical procedural considerations, and an awareness of the balances of power within research

environments during social science fieldwork of all kinds. Feminist research methods are the foundation for my personal considerations of the data included in this book. Analytical tools are necessarily subjective, yet valued for deep insights.

38 See also DuBois (1987) and Freire (1970).

39 Acker, Barry, and Esseveld (1983) argued that research is "embedded in a definite social relationship in which there is a power differential in favor of the knower" even when interviewer and participant share many similarities, though this hopefully lessens the divide due to mutual knowledge and experience (p. 68). There is always a risk as a researcher, the one who will analyze and write up the data (the one with the power to define others' experiences), that a conflict may occur. My inclusion of autoethnographic details in this chapter provides the essential element of recursive meta-analysis of my own conclusions and processes.

40 Attention to the *affect* of research means the consideration of emotional responses to inquiry and recognition that "emotions serve as a source of insight or a signal of rupture in social reality," which may take a positive/caring or negative form (Fonow & Cook, 1991, p. 9).

41 By "constructing emotion as epistemologically subversive, the Western tradition has tended to obscure the vital role of emotion in the construction of knowledge" (Jaggar, 1989, p. 378). Emotions are intentional or cognitive understandings of feelings, which lends some credibility despite the remaining positivist majority of researchers. Jaggar (1989) described emotions as social constructs (individual and involuntary and involving judgments/requiring concepts) and as active engagements that feel involuntary, but can be controlled.

42 Emotion and values are closely related. "Just as values presuppose emotions, so emotions presuppose values" (Jaggar, 1989, p. 383). This speaks to the myth of dispassionate investigation in any research scenario. The problem with the myth of dispassionate inquiry is that it "promotes a conception of epistemological justification vindicating the silencing of...the bearers of emotion...perceived as more 'subjective,' biased, and irrational" (Jaggar, 1989, p. 386).

43 Women are notably absent from Hinojosa's (2010) professional and personal hierarchy. They are devalued as army wives or the military *other*, which translates in terms of masculine identity as *lesser*. The hierarchy of masculinity thus defined depends on categorizing the other in terms of either homosexuality or femininity.

44 My analysis of interview responses incorporated my interpretations of participants' expressions of dimensions of the real, expressions of masculinity in terms of aggression and superiority, and participants' feelings about stereotyping of masculinities (Cole, 2014).

45 Arena analysis is a helpful guiding framework (see Clarke and Montini, 1993), even though my interview data are analyzed using a narrative and pragmatic approach. Arena analysis recommends that there are N sides to any given argument (certainly not just two), and that breaking things down into a binary is not an *innocent* or *meaningless* oversimplification. This approach is relevant to an exploration of identity construction through entertainment like interactive media, because the influences of popular ergodic texts involve more than the immediate players.

46 Acker et al. (1983) described people as "active agents in their own lives," "constructors of their social worlds," yet this activity is not merely individualistic and subjective. It is necessarily "embedded within a set of social

relations" that produces both possibilities and limitations within a given experience (p. 62). If this is the case, then traditional methodology can no longer be viewed as adequate. The use of unstructured or semi-structured interviewing techniques may help elicit talk about personal experiences on the participant's terms rather than the interviewer's.

47 In order to resolve the myriad of complexities and contradictions within feminist methodology, it is necessary to keep in mind the core concepts of interdisciplinarity, intersectionality, reflexivity, and the valuing of experiential knowledge. Unlike positivism, this approach requires emotion and subjectivity.

48 "Situated knowledges imply [that] qualities of multiplicity are locatable in time and space and particular cultures, are embodied in specific ways, and operate as social and collective points of view" (Gottfried, 1996, p. 13).

49 This speaks directly to my argument for interdisciplinary research in Chapter 1 and informs the definition of ergodic ontogeny.

50 Digital media and new media are addressed in *New Media/New Methods: The Academic Turn from Literacy to Electracy* (Rice & O'Gorman, 2008) "by focusing on newness as the process (one might even say, the continual state) of invention, which is the essence of contemporary technological being" (p. 4).

51 Deemer (1967) described a different possibility for expression, a "happening," in which the audience becomes participant. "Clear writing and clear thought follow only after clear experiences, yet the inspiration of such experiences has been virtually neglected by educators" in universities (Deemer, 1967, p. 124).

52 New media theorists often suggest breaking away from old formats. For example, students usually write topic sentences to focus on a concept, but "to be electrate...contemporary writing students need to shift away from thinking in terms of the thing (i.e. the topic sentence)" (Rice & O'Gorman, 2008, p. 282).

53 See questions for commenters on the Vimeo video links that accompany this text. Inclusion of QR Codes provides mobile phone or tablet PC access to embedded videos.

54 MacCannell (1976) argued that "the tour is the only unit of social organization in the modern world that is both suffused with cultural imagery and absolutely detached from surrounding culture" (p. 176). I argue that virtual locations, populations, interactions are similarly fused with and yet separate from culture.

References

Acker, J., Barry, K., & Esseveld, J. (1983). Objectivity and truth: Problems in doing feminist research. *Women's Studies International Forum, 6*, 423–435.

Adler, P. A., & Adler, P. (2002). The reluctant respondent. In J. F. Gubrium & J. A. Holstein (Eds.), *Handbook of interview research: Context & method* (p. 515–536). Thousand Oaks, CA: Sage Publications.

Anderson, D., Jennings Bryant, J., Murray, M., Rivkin, M., & Zillman, D. (2009). Brain imaging: An introduction to a new approach to studying media processes and effects. *Media Psychology, 8*(1), 1–6.

Bhavnani, K. K. (1993). Tracing the contours: Feminist research and feminist objectivity. *Women's Studies International Forum, 16*, 95–104.

Bogost, I. (2016). *Play anything: The pleasure of limits, the uses of boredom, and the secrets of games*. New York, NY: Basic Books.

Bricker, L., & Bell, P. (2012). "'GodMode is his video game name'": Situating learning and identity in structures of social practice. *Cultural Studies of Science Education, 7*(4), 883–902.

Bucholtz, M. (1999). "Why be normal?": Language and identity practices in a community of nerd girls. *Language in Society, 28*(2), 203–223.

Bucholtz, M. (2000). The politics of transcription. *Journal of Pragmatics, 32*(10), 1439–1465.

Clarke, A. (2005). *Situational analysis: Grounded theory after the postmodern turn*. Thousand Oaks, CA: Sage Publications.

Cole, S. M. (2013). Discourses of masculinity: Culture, identity and violence. In D. Boswell, R. O'Shea, & E. Tzadik (Eds.), *Interculturalism, meaning and identity* (p. 153–164). Oxford, UK: Inter-Disciplinary Press.

Cole, S. (2014). Gender identity construction through talk about video games. Special issue: New works on electronic literature and cyberculture. *CLC Web: Comparative Literature and Culture, 15*(16.5). Retrieved from http://dx.doi.org/10.7771/1481-4374.2487.

Collins, P. H. (2000). *Black feminist thought: Knowledge, consciousness, and the politics of empowerment*. New York, NY: Routledge.

Clarke, A., & Montini, T. (1993). The many faces of Ru486: Tales of situated knowledges and technological contestations. *Science, Technology & Human Values, 18*(1), 42–78.

Deemer, C. (1967). English composition as a happening. *College English, 29*(2), 121.

Dietz, N. A., Jones, K. M., Gareau, L., Zeffiro, T. A., & Eden, G. F. (2005). Phonological decoding involves left posterior fusiform gyrus. *Human Brain Mapping, 26*(2), 81–93.

DuBois, W. (1987). *W.E.B. Du Bois writings: The suppression of the African slave-trade/the souls of black folk/dusk of dawn/essays and articles*. New York, NY: Library of America.

Eden, G. F., VanMeter, J. W., Rumsey, J. M., Maisog, J. M., Woods, R. P., & Zeffiro, T. A. (1996). Abnormal processing of visual motion in dyslexia revealed by functional brain imaging. *Nature, 382*(4), 66–69.

Eden, G. F., & Moats, L. (2002). The role of neuroscience in the remediation of students with dyslexia. *Nature Neuroscience, 5*, 1080–1084.

Emerson, R. M., Fretz, R. I., & Shaw, L. L. (1995). *Writing ethnographic fieldnotes*. Chicago, IL: University of Chicago Press.

Enevold, J., & Hagström, C. (2009). Mothers, play and everyday life: Ethnology meets game studies. *Ethnologia Scandinavica, 39*, 27–41.

Farrar, K., Krcmar, M., & McGloin, R. (2013). The perception of human appearance in video games: Toward an understanding of the effects of player perceptions of game features. *Mass Communication & Society, 16*(3), 299–324.

Fonow, M. M., & Cook, J. A. (1991). Back to the future: A look at the second wave of feminist epistemology and methodology. In M. Fonow & J. Cook, *Beyond methodology: Feminist scholarship as lived research* (p. 1–15). Bloomington, IN: Indiana University Press.

Freire, P. (1970). *Pedagogy of the oppressed*. (M. Rasom, trans.). New York, NY: Continuum.

Gee, J. P. (2010). *An introduction to discourse analysis: Theory and method.* New York, NY: Taylor & Francis.

Gong, D., He, H., Liu, D., Ma, W., Dong, L., Luo, C., & Yao, D. (2015). Enhanced functional connectivity and increased gray matter volume of insula related to action video game playing. *Scientific Reports, 5*(9763).

Gottfried, H. (1996). Engaging women's communities: Dilemmas and contradictions in feminist research. In H. Gottfried (Ed.), *Feminism and social change: Bridging theory and practice* (p. 1–20). Chicago, IL: University of Chicago Press.

Granek, J., Gorbet, D., & Sergio, L. (2010). Extensive video-game experience alters cortical networks for complex visuomotor transformations. *Cortex: A Journal Devoted to the Study of the Nervous System & Behavior, 46*(9), 1165–1177.

Griffiths, M. D., Davies, M. & Chappell, D. (2003). Breaking the stereotype: The case of online gaming. *CyberPsychology and Behavior, 6,* 81–91.

Hinojosa, R. (2010). Doing hegemony: Military, men, and constructing a hegemonic masculinity. *The Journal of Men's Studies, 18*(2), 179–194. doi:10.3149/jms.1802.179.

Hsiung, P.-C. (2008). Teaching reflexivity in qualitative interviewing. *Teaching Sociology, 36*(3), 211–226.

Jaggar, A. M. (1989). Love and knowledge: Emotion in feminist epistemology. *Inquiry, 32*(2), 151–176.

Jenkins, H. (2010, June 16). John Fiske: Now and the future. Retrieved from https://civic.mit.edu/blog/henry/john-fiske-now-and-the-future.

Kaplan, A. (1964). *The conduct of inquiry.* Scranton, PA: Chandler.

Kleinman, S., Copp, M. A., & Henderson, K. A. (1997). Qualitatively different: Teaching fieldwork to graduate students. *Journal of Contemporary Ethnography, 25*(4), 469–499.

Landau, E. (2012). What the brain draws from: Art and neuroscience. *CNN.* Retrieved from http://www.cnn.com/2012/09/15/health/art-brain-mind/index.html.

Li, N., Jackson, M. H., & Trees, A. R. (2008). Relating online: Managing dialectical contradictions in massively multiplayer online role-playing game relationships. *Games and Culture: A Journal of Interactive Media, 3*(1), 76–97.

Lorde, A. (1984). Sister outsider: Essays and speeches. Berkeley, CA: Crossing Press.

MacCannell, D. (1976). *The tourist: A new theory of the leisure class.* Los Angeles, CA: University of California Press.

Mani, L. (1990). Multiple mediations: Feminist scholarship in the age of multinational reception. *Feminist Review, 35,* 24–41.

Martin, C. (2012). Video games, identity, and the constellation of information. *Bulletin of Science, Technology & Society, 32*(5), 384–392.

Mathiak, K., & Weber, R. (2006). Toward brain correlates of natural behavior: fMRI during violent video games. *Human Brain Mapping, 27*(12), 948–956.

Mohanty, C. T. (1988). Under western eyes: Feminist scholarship and colonial discourses. *Feminist Review, 30,* 61–88.

Moya, P., & Hames-Garcia, M. (2000). *Reclaiming identity: Realist theory and the predicament of postmodernism.* Los Angeles, CA: University of California Press.

Ong, W. J. (1983). *Orality and literacy: The technologizing of the word.* New York, NY: Methuen.

Patton, M. Q. (2002). *Qualitative research & evaluation methods.* Thousand Oaks, CA: Sage Publications.

Purcell, J. J., Napoliello, E. M., & Eden, G. F. (2011). A combined fMRI study of typed spelling and reading. *NeuroImage, 55*(2), 750–762.

Rice, J., & O'Gorman, M. (Eds.). (2008). *New media/new methods: The academic turn from literacy to electracy.* Anderson, SC: Parlor Press.

Roulston, K. J. (2010). *Reflective interviewing: A guide to theory and practice.* Thousand Oaks, CA: Sage Publications.

Russ, J. (1972). What can a heroine do? Or why women can't write. In. S. Koppelman (Ed.), *Images of women in fiction: Feminist perspectives* (p. 3–20). Bowling Green, OH: Bowling Green University Popular Press.

Scott, J. W. (1986). Gender: A useful category of historical analysis. *The American Historical Review, 91*(5), 1053–1075.

te Wildt, B., Rojas, S., Wedegartner, F., & Szycik, G. (2010). P02–158 emotional responses in excessive players of violent video games: An fMRI-study. *European Psychiatry, 25*(1), 779–779.

Weiss, R. S. (2004). In their own words: Making the most of qualitative interviews. *Contexts, 3*(4), 44–51.

Williams, D., Martins, N., Consalvo, M., & Ivory, J. D. (2009). The virtual census: Representations of gender, race and age in video games. *New Media & Society, 11*(5), 815–834.

Index

9 780367 885366